ENDORSEMENTS FOR
SCRIPTURE AND THE LIFE OF GOD

Scripture and the Life of God goes way beyond being one more informational book on reading Scripture. This book is transformational! Whether a pastor, a long-time discipled Christian, or a novice to the faith, all will be offered a fresh and exciting adventure into the transformational presence and power of God through Holy Scripture. I cannot recommend it highly enough!

—Mike Lowry
Resident Bishop of the Central Texas Conference
of the United Methodist Church

David Watson is a gift to the church today. He combines deep faith, practical instruction, excellent biblical scholarship, and a winsome spirit in producing *Scripture and the Life of God*. In a day when many have forgotten or never learned how to encounter the Bible for personal faith and life development—this book is a gold mine.

—Jeffrey E. Greenway
Lead Pastor at Reynoldsburg United Methodist Church
Reynoldsburg, Ohio

Refreshing and unapologetic guide for Christians to strengthen their faith. Practical steps, replete with scriptural prayers and meditations, to keep the Holy Spirit alive within us. Watson draws upon the rich reservoir of resources available in Scripture and its long history of interpretation.

—Vivian Johnson
Associate Dean for Academic Affairs and
Professor of Old Testament
United Theological Seminary, Dayton, Ohio

The voice of David Watson is consistently clear, relevant, and influential. He is the epitome of insightful, thoughtful, and evangelical scholarship. His view of the Bible as God's "revelation to humanity for the purpose of transformation" is both steeped in our richest theological traditions and as current as breaking news. If David Watson writes it, I recommend it.

—Shane Bishop
Senior Pastor at Christ Church
Fairview Heights, Illinois

Reading *Scripture and the Life of God* was pure joy—as though an excellent Bible scholar was personally walking alongside, explaining the Bible in such clear and understandable language that I was drawn, irresistibly, into deepening desire for a transformational relationship with Scripture. Shared life in God will indeed come alive in any congregation that journeys through these rich pages together.

—Sue Nilson Kibbey
Director, Office of Missional Church Development
West Ohio Conference of the United Methodist Church

The most important thing I do as a pastor is to help my people read Scripture. There's a problem, though: Scripture can be difficult and intimidating. *Scripture and the Life of God* by

David Watson addresses that problem. In it, Watson provides a helpful introduction to Scripture and addresses many of the concerns that people have about the Bible. This is a book I'll be putting in the hands of folks in my church.

—Andrew Forrest
Pastor, Munger Place Church, Dallas, Texas

Scripture

AND THE

Life

OF

G✠D

Scripture
AND THE
Life
OF
G✠D

Why the Bible Matters Today
More Than Ever

David F. Watson

 Seedbed

Printed in the United States of America

Cover design by Strange Last Name
Page design by PerfecType, Nashville, Tennessee

Watson, David F., 1970-
  Scripture and the life of God : why the Bible matters today more than ever / David F. Watson. – Frankin, Tennessee : Seedbed Publishing, ©2017.

  pages ; cm.

  1. A path into the life of God – 2. Reading for the life of God – 3. Guides into the life of God – 4. Expectation and the life of God. – 5. One book for the life of God.
  Includes bibliographical references (pages).
  ISBN 9781628244724 (paperback : alk. paper)
  ISBN 9781628244731 (Mobi)
  ISBN 9781628244748 (ePub)
  ISBN 9781628244755 (uPDF)

  1. Bible--Inspiration. 2. Bible--Evidences, authority, etc. 3. Bible--Reading. 4. God--Knowableness. 5. Spiritual formation. 6. Spiritual exercises. I. Title.

BS480.W38 2017   220.1   2017952693

 Seedbed

SEEDBED PUBLISHING
Franklin, Tennessee
seedbed.com

For Harriet, Luke, and Sean

CONTENTS

ACKNOWLEDGMENTS

I am exceedingly grateful to my wife, Harriet, for reading drafts of these chapters, providing feedback, and putting up with me in general. It's not always a cakewalk dealing with an academic whose nose is glued to a book or eyes are fixed on a computer screen. This book probably would not have been written without her help, and even if I had managed to complete the manuscript single-handedly, it would have been a much more tedious and tiresome work. Any tedious or tiresome elements that remain are entirely my fault.

Amanda Moseng, my research assistant, provided tremendous help in tracking down sources, formatting, and giving feedback on specific chapters. She also wrote the study questions at the end of each chapter. Unfortunately (for me), she will graduate at the end of this semester, and there is apparently nothing I can do about it. I despair that I will not find so capable of an assistant for years to come.

Phyllis Ennist, one of my colleagues at United Theological Seminary, read an early draft of this work and offered helpful feedback. I am grateful not only for the time she spent in reading the manuscript, but her honesty, which is both refreshing and humbling.

My mother and father, Valrie and David Watson, also read early drafts of chapters and gave feedback. They were, as I would expect, candid about which parts made sense, which didn't, and which were not particularly readable. This feedback has been invaluable. I certainly didn't want to write a book that no one would want to read, and I knew that, as my parents, they would tell me were I writing such a book.

The idea for this book, that Scripture is a port of entry into the life of God, began years ago in conversations with Billy Abraham and Jason Vickers. Our work together on the Canonical Theism project was deeply formative for me, and I will always appreciate the opportunity to have been a part of it.

There are many conversation partners who have helped to refine my ideas as iron sharpens iron. There are simply too many to name, though I should mention Drew McIntyre and Joel Watts, who took the time to read sections of this work and provided both critique and affirmation. I also want to acknowledge my colleagues at United Theological Seminary who are so deeply committed not only to the life of the mind, but to the formation of faithful Christian leaders in service to Christ and the church. My time at United has shaped me in important ways. These colleagues have challenged me, encouraged me, and taken me down a peg when I needed it. I have been blessed at United not only by the opportunity to pursue my scholarly and ecclesial interests, but with Christian friendships.

Finally, many thanks to Andrew Miller and J. D. Walt at Seedbed for believing in this project and offering extremely helpful suggestions for improvement. I am grateful to work with Seedbed, a publisher dedicated to producing high-quality work that serves Christ and the church.

INTRODUCTION

"Pick up and read. . . . Pick up and read. . . ." It was the voice of a child, chanting these words over and over again, that caught Augustine's attention. He had run toward God, and then away. He had loved God and resisted God at the same time. He had struggled mightily with sin, both enchanted and repulsed by his own desires. He was in agony, in tears even, his heart divided between a life dedicated to himself and a life dedicated to God.

As he heard the words *Pick up and read* coming from a nearby house, he took this as a divine command to open the Scriptures and read the first chapter he might find. "I seized it," he wrote, "opened it and in silence read the first passage on which my eyes lit: 'Not in riots and drunken parties, not in eroticism and indecencies, not in strife and rivalry, but put on the Lord Jesus Christ and make no provision for the flesh in its lusts' (Rom. 13:13–14)." At that moment, the storm raging in his heart became quiet. "At once, with the last words of this sentence, it was as if a light of relief from all anxiety flooded into my heart. All the shadows of doubt were dispelled."[1]

Through these words of Scripture, Augustine took a crucial step forward in his relationship with God. He had kept God at arm's length, but now he welcomed the warm embrace of the true source of love, joy, and peace. He now knew God in a new way. A relationship with God, after all, is in some ways like any other relationship. We cannot have a meaningful relationship with someone we keep pushing away. On the contrary, a real relationship requires that two people enter into one another's lives, that they become a *part* of one another's lives. They will inevitably be changed in the process. If we are changed by our relationships with other people, how much more so with God?

Entering into the life of God is like walking into the ocean. The further you go, the more immersed you become. You become more aware of its overwhelming power, its vastness and mystery. The difference is that if you walk too deeply into the ocean you will die, but walking deeply into the life of God brings life. When we are immersed in the life of God, we begin to experience new life in the here and now. Our desires, our character, the way in which we regard ourselves and other people—all of these change. As John Wesley put it, "And what is righteousness but the life of God in the soul, the mind which was in Christ Jesus, the image of God stamped upon the heart, now renewed after the likeness of him that created it?"[2] This newness of life does not end when our physical bodies die, but extends into eternity. Through Christ, we are able to experience the love of God forever. The life of God never ends, and we are being drawn into that divine life.

Divine Communication

The problem is, while God is always reaching out to us to draw us into relationship, on our own we do not know how to respond, or even why we should. We don't know how to return God's love. Yes, we can learn things about God by observing the world around us. We might perceive, for example, that God is creative. The very existence of the universe testifies to this. We might see that God values order over chaos given the ordered nature of the world in which we live. We might conclude that God is good because of the beauty of the world, and because of such qualities of life as friendship, love, and joy. This kind of understanding is based on what is often called "natural revelation." There are truths about God that we can grasp simply by observation of the natural world.

Natural revelation, however, only reveals a very general picture of God. It's kind of like seeing a figure at a great distance. You can make out that the figure is that of a person, and maybe even some details about that person. You might judge, for example, that this person is a woman, and perhaps how tall she is. You can make out the color of her clothes. Apart from this, however, you know very little. You need to get to know her better. You need to have a conversation with her, spend time with her, and hear her story. And as you do, you will be drawn into her life, and she into yours. You will, in other words, form a relationship.

To form a relationship with God, we need to know not just the general things, but the particulars of the divine life. We can derive these particulars from what is often called "special revelation," and the most important source of special revelation Christians have is the Bible. So, for example, by observing the world around you, you might know that there is a God who is creative and good. You would not, however, derive that this God acted powerfully through the people of Israel. You would not know that this same God came to us in Jesus Christ, or that this God so loved the world that he gave his only Son, so that whoever believes in him will not perish, but will have eternal life (John 3:16). You might perceive that God values order over chaos, but you would not perceive that this same God gave Ten Commandments to Moses (Exodus 20:1–17), or that in Christ, God was reconciling the world to himself (2 Corinthians 5:19). We require the special divine revelation that is in Scripture in order to grasp these truths.[3]

We need to know who the true God is and what this God has done for us. We need to know this because the divine gift of salvation is more important than anything else that people can receive, and our very eternal lives depend upon it. There is danger here because we are so easily led astray. John Calvin famously remarked that the human mind is an idol-making factory. Different views of the world generally bring with them different views of truth. For some, science holds the highest and most important truths we can grasp. For others, truth is a particular philosophical or religious system that they share with a community of like-minded people.

It is also quite common for people today to see truth as a primarily individualistic affair: "I decide my own truth." Once we say this, however, we lose the very idea of a broader truth woven into the fabric of creation. This outlook is typical within what we call our present "postmodern" era. As Andrew G. Walker and Robin A. Parry wrote in their book, *Deep Church Rising*, today "one is more likely to come across the idea that nobody is right or wrong" on questions of religious truth. There may be such truth, "but it is person-relative." Each of us decides truth for ourselves. No one can judge us because "each individual has the right to make such decisions."[4]

Christians, however, can't really believe this way. Jesus said that he came to testify to the truth (John 18:37). Pilate, who was interrogating him, asked a question people were asking long before him, and continue to ask today: "What is truth?" (John 18:38). Christians know that *God* is truth. Whatever else we say is true is somehow ultimately rooted in God. Science and math may tell us true things, but God is the source of the laws of science and math. As people of faith we make truth claims about right and wrong, knowing that God called into being the moral fabric of the universe. God is truth, and once we recognize this, all of the smaller quests for truth in our life are actually quests to understand the divine.

Left on our own, we cannot truly know God, but we are not on our own. God has revealed himself to us in history, and our primary resource for receiving God's self-revelation is the Bible. Our faith, then, stands over against the idea that there is no truth, as well as truth claims incompatible with ours made by other religions and philosophies, such as Buddhism or atheism.

Two words of caution are in order here. First, to claim that we can know true things about God is not to claim that we are immune to mistakes or that we know the *whole* truth about God. God is eternal, and we are finite. God is Spirit, and we spend most of our time in the this-world matters of everyday life. In some ways, our vision may be distorted by sin, by the limitations of our intellect, or by assumptions about God that we may not even be aware that we hold. As Paul said, "For now we see only a reflection as in a mirror; then we shall see face to face. Now I know in part; then I shall know fully, even as I am fully known" (1 Cor. 13:12). In my own life as a Christian, there have been many times when I've come to see things differently than I did before. I've changed my mind or, perhaps, God changed my mind. I've realized I've been wrong about things, and I'm reasonably sure this will happen again in the future. It has therefore become ever more important for me to rely on other believers—past and present—for guidance, a topic we will take up in chapter 3.

Second, knowing the truth about God is not enough. As we read in James 2:19, even the demons believe (and tremble). Believing is necessary, but it is not sufficient. John Wesley once quipped that a person could be as "orthodox as the devil," and "all the while be as great a stranger as he to the religion of the heart."[5] You can believe all the right things about God and still not know God. You can recite any creed you would like and yet not know the transforming power of the Holy Spirit. Knowing the basic truths about God that

Christians have confessed through the centuries is necessary, but not sufficient. It is crucial, but it is not enough. When we read the Bible, then, we should look not just for *information* about God, but for the *transformation* that comes from God. The Bible isn't just a book of statements *about* God; it is a pathway into God's very life.

This function of the Bible seems to have been lost in much of Christianity through North America and Western Europe. In the mainline Protestant traditions, and increasingly in evangelicalism, we have gotten very good at being critical of the Bible. We have become experts in defeating the bogeyman of biblical literalism, so much so that "critical" has become the primary posture by which we approach the text. Joel Green put the matter this way: "[M]odern persons who think of themselves as Christians and who identify themselves with the Christian church have often been enculturated to imagine not only that they *can* but indeed that they *must* approach the Scriptures dispassionately."[6] Thus we live our lives at a safe distance from those passages of the Bible that are most challenging to us, and perhaps those through which God can shape us most profoundly. Our abbreviated Bible becomes a reflection of our own perspectives, and the idea of God becomes an empty bucket that we fill up with the values of our culture.

We have little to say about the role of God in the writing of Scripture and selection of the books of the Bible (the canon). We are most often reticent to talk about the work of the Holy Spirit in guiding our readings. Put differently, we don't have much to say about the Bible theologically. I was once part of a process of interviewing candidates for a professorial position in teaching the Bible. One of the other interviewers, a professor of theology, asked each candidate one simple question: "What is the Bible?" It surprised me that, despite the great learning and intelligence of each of these candidates, every one of them struggled to answer this question.

My guess is that many Christians in North America and Western Europe—including the best educated among them—would struggle with this question as well. They would have a hard time saying not only what the Bible *is*, but what it is supposed to do. Yes, they could probably muster some formula such as, "The Bible is the Word of God," or, "The Bible teaches us how to live a Christian life." Yet these common ways of describing the Bible don't tell us much about it at all.

To put the matter differently, we have lost sight of the Bible as *Scripture*.[7] What does it mean to think of the Bible as Scripture? Daniel Castello and Robert Wall put the matter this way: "'Scripture' signals a way of thinking theologically about the Bible as God's Word for God's people, one that supplies the theological goods that fund spiritual wisdom and provide moral direction."[8] Another way of putting this is to say that, through the Bible, God has revealed sacred truth to a community of people committed to living in that truth. The traditional tools of biblical scholars, such as the biblical languages, historical study, and literary analysis, contribute in important ways to our understanding of the Bible. Nevertheless, one can achieve outstanding mastery of these tools and never read the Bible as *Scripture*.

It's common to find academic biblical studies that approach the Bible in the same way they might approach, say, *The Odyssey*. They do not assume the reality of the God to whom the Bible attests, nor do they assume that God had any role in the writing or selection of the biblical texts. From this perspective, the Bible is simply one more example of ancient religious literature. There is a certain logic to approaching the Bible in this way in a secular context such as a state university classroom. In the Sunday school or seminary classroom, however, such an approach will inevitably be inadequate. We are not reading the Bible simply to learn about history. We are reading it to deepen our relationship with Jesus Christ, to enter more deeply into the divine life. As Christians, we should feel free and comfortable to approach the Bible with our core theological truths in hand. In fact, we should feel uncomfortable *not* doing so. Only then will we be able to receive the spiritual treasures that Scripture has to offer.

In this book, I want to argue a singular point: the Bible is a form of divine communication meant to lead us more fully into the life of God. Put in theological terms, we might say that through the Bible we receive divine revelation, the purpose of which is soteriological. In other words, the purpose of God's Word is salvation for the world. John Wesley believed that Scripture shows us "the way to heaven—how to land safe on that happy shore. . . . Here then I am, far from the busy ways of men. I sit down alone: only God is here. In his presence I open, I read his Book; for this end, to find the way to heaven."[9] Or to put it in yet another way, God speaks to us through the Bible and leads us into salvation. God loves us and wishes us to return that love. When we do, we enter more fully into the divine life. The Bible is a "book of meeting."[10] It draws us ever more deeply into a relationship with the God who came to us in Jesus Christ. In light of this, our first posture toward the Bible should be one of gratitude, not criticism.

Scripture and Renewal

Quite often we hear calls for renewal in the church and ideas about the best way for this to happen. Yes, the renewal of the church is a good idea. But if the church needs renewing, it is in part because it has been ineffective in its job of making saints. Put differently, people themselves are not being renewed, and in the absence of cultural Christendom in the West they see no reason to participate in the life of a church that does not offer them something truly powerful, something that will change their lives. I once heard the evangelist Larry Randolph say that the problem with church renewal in the United States is that we want the *power* of God without the *character* of God. We want to see signs and wonders. We want our churches to grow and our congregations to thrive. What we don't truly want, he said, is to be changed by God, to have the pride and self-will and sin burned out of our lives by the power of the Holy Spirit. True renewal will come when we seek not only the power of God, but the character of God.

God is a great physician, we are the patients, and God's medicine bag is the church. Within the church, we hold the delicate instruments by which God heals our wounds, our sin, our brokenness. The faith passed down through the centuries, our practices of worship, our common prayers and confessions of faith, and, yes, the Bible, are means by which God applies the medicine of the Holy Spirit. Yet if we neglect the medicine of the Holy Spirit or use the gifts of the Spirit wrongly, we deprive ourselves and others of the surest means of receiving the healing balm of divine grace. It matters, then, how we pray. The faith we confess matters. The way in which we receive Holy Communion makes a difference. And most assuredly, the way that we read Scripture matters as well. The attitudes we assume, our practices of reading, the assumptions we bring to the text, and our expectations of God's work through the Bible will come to bear on our spiritual well-being.

There are many books on how to read the Bible. This book is as much about *why* as it is about *how*. We read the Bible with an intentional openness to God's work of healing because we are broken by sin and we need to be made whole. Our lives are imperfect, sometimes painful, sometimes joyful, always broken apart from Christ. That is the nature of human existence. God's life is perfect. It is whole. It is eternal. That is the nature of God's existence. You and

I, broken as we are, are invited into the life of God so that we can be healed. This is why God has given us the Bible.

This is a book written by a Christian for Christians. If others read it, I do hope they find it both enjoyable and edifying. This book, however, takes a specifically confessional stance toward Scripture. In what follows, I don't attempt to adopt some type of neutral stance that can speak to any range of religious and ideological positions. Rather, I'm writing unapologetically out of a commitment to the Great Tradition of Christian faith (sometimes called the Nicene-Chalcedonian tradition). In fact, one of my more important intellectual commitments is that Christian scholars should speak *as* Christians. They should be no less intellectually rigorous, no less discerning, and they should not simply turn off their critical faculties. Nevertheless, the faith we confess on Sunday morning should shape the way we perceive every aspect of our lives. As Paul says in 2 Corinthians 10:5, "We demolish arguments and every pretension that sets itself up against the knowledge of God, and we take captive every thought to make it obedient to Christ." Our *every thought* should be obedient to Christ. Being a Christian is not just a way of behaving, nor is it simply a way of thinking about God. It involves a set of commitments that should shape the way in which we see everything—our neighbors, our bodies, our money, our work, and if we are scholars, our scholarship.

In what follows we will explore several ways of approaching the Bible that can facilitate our growth in faith. In chapter 1, we will look at what it means to be drawn into the life of God through the Bible, a topic that will involve a brief foray into the subjects of inspiration and authority. Chapter 2 will take up the idea that there are ways of reading the Bible that are more and less helpful for the life of faith. Prayer, meditation, song, and ritual are all means by which we can draw upon the deep resources of Scripture. In chapter 3, we will examine the ways in which the community of faith, both past and present, can aid us in our reading. Chapter 4 will take up the ways in which the mighty works of God and the unseen world disclosed in Scripture can form our expectations today. The fifth and final chapter will discuss what is called the "canonicity" of the Bible. That is to say, we will look at the ways in which the *whole* Bible, from start to finish, contributes to our journey into the life of God. My hope is that, as you make your way through these chapters, the Holy Spirit will move you to a greater awareness and deeper appreciation of the Bible as a resource to help us know, love, and follow the one and only living God.

CHAPTER 1

A PATH INTO THE LIFE OF GOD

When I was a graduate student, I taught in a publicly funded community college as a part-time instructor. One of the courses I taught was "Bible as Literature." Since I had little money and even less teaching experience, I was happy to have some kind of academic job. I enjoyed interacting with the students and, of course, I was very interested in the subject matter. What I didn't like, however, was that I couldn't speak about the Bible from a *confessional* perspective. Put differently, I couldn't speak as a Christian. I understood the reasons for this and did my best to maintain a position of neutrality in the classroom, but it always felt like something was missing, that I wasn't allowed to give the whole story.

Of course, something *was* missing because the Bible was never meant to be simply an object of study detached from its religious significance. The Bible, from its very beginnings, is supposed to teach us about the God we worship and that same God's work among us for salvation. It is, after all, the church's book, and the Christians who assembled the collection of works that form our Bible did so in order to teach the saving faith of the church. Yes, people use the Bible for all kinds of purposes—for example, to make money, as an object of study, or to manipulate. From the earliest days of our faith, though,

Christians have considered particular writings scriptural because they help us to grow as people of faith. In other words, they draw us into the life of God. In this chapter, we will look at what entry into the life of God means. We will consider why the Bible can do this when so many other books cannot, which will involve a trek into the forests of the inspiration of Scripture and the authority of Scripture.

Entering into the Life of God

I begin with a basic assertion of Christian faith: human beings are broken. I'm not talking about some human beings. I mean everyone. We are broken. In the Christian tradition, we have normally called this brokenness "sin." We don't always act the way we should. We catch ourselves thinking things we don't want to think. Sometimes we are too hard on other people. Sometimes we are too hard on ourselves. It's as Paul described in Romans 7:15–19:

> I do not understand what I do. For what I want to do I do not do, but what I hate I do. And if I do what I do not want to do, I agree that the law is good. As it is, it is no longer I myself who do it, but it is sin living in me. For I know that good itself does not dwell in me, that is, in my sinful nature. For I have the desire to do what is good, but I cannot carry it out. For I do not do the good I want to do, but the evil I do not want to do—this I keep on doing.

Even if we know what is right, and even if we want to do what is right, we don't always do it. That's the human condition. First John 1:8–10 testifies to this as well: "If we claim to be without sin, we deceive ourselves and the truth is not in us. If we confess our sins, he is faithful and just and will forgive us our sins and purify us from all unrighteousness. If we claim we have not sinned, we make him out to be a liar and his word is not in us."

Despite our many imperfections, though, we are not given over to despair. God wishes to rescue us from this condition by dwelling within us, filling us with the Holy Spirit, and changing us from the inside out. The poet Francis Thompson spoke of God as the "hound of heaven," relentless in the pursuit of men and women who seek to fill the empty space in their lives with earthly pleasures. We don't have to live apart from God. When Christ died on the cross, the vise-grip of sin upon our lives was broken, and we have the opportunity to live in a new way now with God's help. We can know what is right, will what is right, and do what is right. God makes this possible. But to live in this way, we must enter ever more fully into the life of God.

The Life of God and Salvation

What does it mean to be taken into the life of God? This is simply another way of talking about salvation. To understand this, we have to know something about the nature of the God we worship. The Christian God is Father, Son, and Holy Spirit—the Holy Trinity. As theologian Kathryn Tanner explained it, "From the Father, through the Son, in the Spirit, is the world created, saved, and brought to its end."[1] God the Father loves God the Son, who in turn loves God the Father, and the two are bound together in community and love by God the Holy Spirit. *God exists eternally as a communion of divine love.*

We were made to participate in the divine love of God, but sin prevents us from doing so. Sin puts us at a great distance from the love of God, and it even confuses us so that we can't find our way back. Through his work on the cross, however, Jesus builds for us a road that leads back to God. The further we walk along this road, the more we can experience the love of God. The Holy Spirit takes our hand and acts as our guide. If we are tempted to turn back, to take a detour, or simply stop where we are, the Holy Spirit leads us on. Thus we can participate in the mutual love of the Holy Trinity. God the Holy Spirit leads us through God the Son into communion with God the Father.

When we encounter God in this way, we cannot help but be changed. The love of God begins to renew our minds (Romans 12:2). We think differently. We see the world differently. We are no longer compelled to abide by our old patterns of living, but rather become a new kind of person. The lyrics to the Christian hymn "Spirit of the Living God" describe this process beautifully: "Spirit of the living God, fall afresh on me / Melt me, mold me, fill me, use me."[2] We want God to do all of these things so that we can become the people we are meant to be. In some traditions, this is called "sanctification," or being made holy. In the Orthodox tradition, it is called "theosis," or being made more like God. Second Peter describes it this way:

> [God's] divine power has given us everything we need for a godly life through our knowledge of him who called us by his own glory and goodness. Through these he has given us his very great and precious promises, so that through them you may participate in the divine nature, having escaped the corruption in the world caused by evil desires. (1:3–4)

It may be hard to believe, but you and I have the precious opportunity to participate in the divine nature. The very idea is almost incomprehensible, but it is nonetheless true.

The fourth-century theologian Athanasius described it this way: "[God], indeed, assumed humanity that we might become God."[3] We have to be careful here not to misinterpret this statement. Athanasius didn't mean that we become the same as the eternal God who created the universe. He meant that God gives us something that, on our own, we do not and cannot have. You and I can partake of the divine nature. Those who encounter God this way become different people. Their desires change. Their wills change. Their very thoughts are different than they were before. They don't feel entirely at home in this world anymore. First Peter tells us that we who follow Jesus are aliens and exiles (2:11) because our primary citizenship is no longer of this world, but within the kingdom of God. Though the world cannot see it, we are a royal priesthood, a holy nation (2:9). Once we were no people, but now we are God's people (2:10). We are drawn into the life of God, and we are thereby changed.

Reading Scripture for Its Intended Purpose

From the earliest days of the faith, believers have understood that knowing who the true God is and what this God has done for our salvation guides us more fully into the love of God. We are not saved by this knowledge; we are only saved by the work of Christ. Yet this knowledge leads us to accept God's great gift for us. It leads us to trust our lives, both present and eternal, to God. It shows God's love for us and creates faith within us. Reading the Bible can lead to knowledge of God, and knowledge of God can lead to salvation. As Paul wrote in Romans 10:13–14, "for, 'Everyone who calls on the name of the Lord will be saved.' How, then, can they call on the one they have not believed in? And how can they believe in the one of whom they have not heard?" We learn about the good news of God through the message of salvation given over to us in Scripture. True knowledge of God can lead us to salvation, and we should therefore attend carefully to the ways in which the Bible teaches us about God's saving work in history.[4]

Of course, anyone who can read, can read the Bible, but not everyone will read it according to its intended purpose. We see an extreme example of this in the atheist Richard Dawkins, who wrote, "The God of the Old Testament is arguably the most unpleasant character in all fiction: jealous and proud of it; a petty, unjust, unforgiving control-freak; a vindictive, bloodthirsty ethnic cleanser; a misogynistic, homophobic, racist, infanticidal, geno-cidal, filicidal, pestilential, megalomaniacal, sadomasochistic, capriciously malevolent bully."[5] Dawkins at the very least knew some stories of the Bible well enough to form a caricature of the God of the Old Testament. He used this caricature to argue against belief in the God of Jewish and Christian faith. He was not the first to use the Bible in this way, nor will he be the last. The ways in which people use the Bible and their reasons for doing so are many and varied, and sometimes evil.

The Christian Bible is a gift given by God through the church, to the church. It is the church's book. Others may use it. Others will surely read it, but only those who will give themselves over to the God revealed in its pages can use the Bible in the way in which it was intended. We have received this gift so that we can know and love God, and enter more deeply into the faith of the church. As Christopher Bryan wrote, "[T]hrough scripture God invites us into God's heart."[6] That is why the early followers of Jesus used the Scriptures of Israel. That is why early Christians began to read and revere some specifically Christian writings as having the same status as the Scriptures of Israel. That is why they began to form collections of writings, including some works and laying others aside. We have the Bible to help us know and love God, and no other writing or collection of writings can do this in the same way or to the same degree.

The Divine Inspiration of the Bible

If we believe that Scripture is a gift from God to lead us into salvation, it only makes sense to say that God has guided the writings of Scripture in order to provide us with the teaching we need. Christians, therefore, affirm that the Bible is divinely inspired. This is a place where our language trips us up a bit. The New International Version translation of the Bible is helpful in its rendering of 2 Timothy 3:16: "All Scripture is God-breathed and is useful for teaching, rebuking, correcting and training in righteousness."[7] The Greek word *theopneustos* ("God-breathed" or "inspired") is very uncommon in Greek literature. In fact, the use of it in 2 Timothy is its first known appearance.[8] Because it is such an uncommon word, it is hard for us to translate. We don't have very much context to help us ascertain what ancient Greek-speaking people might have understood by it. It seems clear, though, that by saying Scripture was "God-breathed," 2 Timothy affirms that the Spirit of God came to bear in a significant way on the writings that together make up the Bible.

Exactly *how* did the Spirit come to bear on these writings? That's the million-dollar question, sometimes even among Christians within the same community. Almost all Christians believe that Scripture is a reliable guide, given to us by God, to teach us what we need to know about salvation. Beyond this, we enter into a briar patch of theories about how God inspired the biblical writers, how the teachings of Scripture relate to fields of knowledge like science and history, and the extent to which the words of Scripture have been reliably preserved through the centuries. I personally think these kinds of questions are both interesting and important, but they are too complex to pursue in this chapter. (And, to be honest, many people find them a bit dry.)

The Purpose of Inspiration

The Bible itself, however, is less concerned with a particular theory of inspiration than it is with telling us the purpose of inspiration. Second Timothy, for example, does not tell us exactly what it means for Scripture to be "God-breathed," but it does provide a statement of what Scripture does *because* it is God-breathed:[9]

> But as for you, continue in what you have learned and have become convinced of, because you know those from whom you learned it, and how from infancy you have known the Holy Scriptures, which are able to make you wise for salvation through faith in Christ Jesus. All Scripture is God-breathed and is useful for teaching, rebuking, correcting and training in righteousness, so that the servant of God may be thoroughly equipped for every good work. (3:14–17)

Historically speaking, this passage has to do with the writings that Christians call the Old Testament. The New Testament, after all, had not yet come into being. It would be a mistake, however, to suggest that these words about inspiration do not apply to the New Testament as well. Followers of Jesus and the early Christians first understood the Jewish Bible as Scripture—as an authoritative work given by God to the community of faith for our well-being. Over time, Christians began to accord other writings—specifically Christian writings—that same status. Yet it makes no sense to accord these newer writings the same status as the Jewish Bible if we do not believe that they come from the same Source and serve the same purpose. The same Spirit who inspired the Old Testament inspired the New. If God intended the writings of the New Testament to stand alongside those of the Old Testament as Scripture, then what is said about the inspiration of one should apply to the other.

We learn from this passage several ways in which God has inspired Scripture in order to help us.[10] Scripture is able to make us wise for salvation through faith in Christ. It is "useful for teaching, rebuking, correcting, and training in righteousness." These qualities of Scripture are for the purpose of equipping the servants of God for the good works they will do. Through Scripture, we are to learn about salvation and righteousness so that we can be about God's work in the world. The alignment of our will with God's is part of our journey into the divine life.

God teaches the community of believers in many different ways, such as through preaching, prophecy, and the writings of great teachers and thinkers. Scripture, however, has a unique function related to teaching within the church. It is a touchstone, a standard against which other teachings are measured. If I were to claim, for example, that God told me to spend all of my money on myself and give none of it to others, the people of my faith community could rightly respond that this "prophecy" violates the teachings of Scripture (for example, Deuteronomy 15:7–11; Luke 6:38; James 2:15–16). What I believe that God had told me does not measure up to the standard that God has given for teaching in the community of faith. Hence, it is likely to lead me away from the life of God, rather than more deeply into it. It is also likely to hurt the community of faith, rather than help it.

Is Scripture a Unique Standard?

Occasionally one comes across notions of inspiration that diminish Scripture's role as a standard for sound teaching. For example, Adam Hamilton, in his book *Making Sense of the Bible*, argued,

> [T]he Bible's authors were inspired by the Spirit *in the same way and to the same degree* as many contemporary preachers and

prophets and even ordinary Christians have been inspired by the Spirit in every age. You've likely felt moved by the Spirit, and you've likely heard God speak to you as you listened to a sermon or a song, or read an inspirational book. I believe the inspiration experienced by the biblical authors was not different from our own experience of inspiration.[11]

Taking this approach, there is no theological reason that the witness of Scripture should carry more weight than experiences of the Spirit that you or I might have. In other words, from this perspective, the Bible is inspired, but not *uniquely* inspired.

Hamilton's notion of inspiration represents quite a departure from some of the important claims that Christians have made about Scripture through the centuries. Throughout almost every branch of Christianity one finds the belief that, in our Scriptures, we have a unique self-revelation from God. It was given to guide first Israel and then the church in the ways of truth and righteousness. From the early centuries of our faith, Christians have held that the Bible serves as a standard—a measuring rod, or canon—against which we can assess what is taught in the church, as well as individual thoughts, words, and deeds. We have held that the Bible has unique authority because God has given it to us in order to function in this way. If the inspiration of Scripture is no different from the way in which you or I might be inspired today, it is difficult to see why we should consider Scripture to be a standard at all. In chapter 5 we will look at the concept of Scripture as canon in more detail.

The Work of God through the Whole Formation of the Bible

Whatever notion of inspiration we adopt, it is important to understand that God has been at work through the whole process of the Bible's formation. Most of the time, when we think about the inspiration of Scripture, we think about the ways in which God guided the people who wrote the Bible.[12] It is a mistake, however, to limit the work of God in the inspiration of Scripture *only* to the writers. Paul Achtemeier argued that the biblical writers and editors "regularly used traditions that had been formulated prior to the composition of the book in which they came to be included."[13] It would be common for biblical writers to include ideas they had received from their communities of faith.

For example, in 1 Corinthians 15, Paul wrote to the church in Corinth about the message they had received from him. He himself, he said, received this message from others:

> that Christ died for our sins according to the Scriptures, that he was buried, that he was raised on the third day according to the Scriptures, and that he appeared to Cephas, and then to the Twelve. After that, he appeared to more than five hundred of the brothers and sisters at the same time, most of whom are still living, though some have fallen asleep. Then he appeared to James, then to all the apostles. (vv. 3–7)

While Paul did receive revelations directly from God (Galatians 1:11–12), it seems here he is emphasizing truths about Jesus that he had learned in the church.

Likewise, in Hebrews we read of the message of salvation, "which was first announced by the Lord, [and] was confirmed to us by those who heard him. God also testified to it by signs, wonders and various miracles, and by gifts of the Holy Spirit distributed according to his will" (2:3–4). The writer is talking in this passage about an understanding of the gospel that was handed down from the people who heard Jesus himself.

Achtemeier continued, "The close interrelationship of Scripture and community . . . means that the inspiration of the biblical materials began already with the first formulation of those traditions, and continued as they were reshaped and reformulated during their transmission within the ongoing community."[14] To put this more simply, he was saying that God guided the beliefs of the Israelite and Christian communities even before those beliefs were written down in Scripture. He urged us to think of inspiration as something that began long before the biblical writings themselves were written, compiled, and collected into the Bible. God inspired the communities of faith that formulated and shaped the traditions that eventually became biblical.

Achtemeier's perspective brings us to a related idea called "concursive action." This is simply a term theologians use to say that, at every level of its formation, the Bible has been the product of divine and human cooperation. As I. Howard Marshall put it, "the Scriptures can be seen on one level as the work of the Spirit and on another level as the work of human authors."[15] The work of the Spirit extends through the whole process of composition: "the collection of information from witnesses, the use of written sources, the writing up and editing of such information, the composition of spontaneous letters, the committing to writing of prophetic messages, the collecting of the various documents together, and so on."[16] From the first ideas that gave rise to the Scriptures to the much later decisions about which books to include and which to leave out, God has been at work in, through, and with human beings.

Scripture Makes Sense of Our Lives

In most churches, people could tell you in general terms what their church or denomination says about the Bible. They might say, "We believe it's true, cover to cover," or "We believe the Bible is true in all of the important things about salvation, but it might not provide a scientifically accurate account of creation." In some more liberal churches, you might hear people say something like, "We don't take the Bible literally, but we believe that it teaches us important universal truths about life." No doubt one could find many other variations as well. They may not, however, know the very specific teaching of their church or denomination. For example, I would doubt that many people in the tradition that I belong to, the United Methodist Church, know that we have official statements on the nature of and function of Scripture, such as the following:

> The Holy Scripture containeth all things necessary to salvation; so that whatsoever is not read therein, nor may be proved thereby, is not to be required of any man that it should be believed as an article of faith, or be thought requisite or necessary to salvation. In the name of the Holy Scripture we do understand those canonical books of the Old and New Testament of whose authority was never any doubt in the church.[17]

This is the kind of statement that tends to be meaningful to theologians, and perhaps to pastors, but most laypeople don't lie awake at night thinking about it. Why not? The reason is that, for most Christians, Scripture is meaningful not because of some notion of inspiration, but because of the real ways in which it speaks into our lives and makes sense of our existence.

On my shelf I have my grandmother's old Bible. It is a small, unassuming black book, a red-letter King James Version. On the back side of the title page she wrote, "Psalms 27:14: Wait on the Lord: be of good courage and he shall strengthen thine heart: Wait, I say, on the Lord. Given to David, my grandson, with love. Grandmother. June 11, 1990." She was eighty-eight years old when she gave me that Bible. She had seen a life of great hardship. Her father was a hard and mean man and her mother withdrawn and passive. She had lived through poverty and relentless work in cotton fields when she was young. When she was older she worked as a night nurse. Her husband and oldest son both experienced severe burns while working, and her husband died when they were in their forties after he was hit by a car. She raised seven children, sometimes with only oil, flour, and potatoes to eat, if even that. She gave birth to my father when she was forty-one years old, and she was in her seventies by the time I began to develop memories of her.

"Wait on the Lord: be of good courage and he shall strengthen thine heart." Of all the passages she could have inscribed in this Bible, she chose this one. Is it difficult to see why? Through one hardship after another, she was upheld by faith in God. She knew and lived the words she wrote. She knew a God who would strengthen her heart. These words of the Bible bolstered her. They made sense to her. Life did not always make sense, but these words did.

Part of why I trust the Bible is because I have seen so many people, like my grandmother, who have been sustained by its words. And, following in their example, I have been as well. My life has been easy compared to my grandmother's, but every life has hardship. Every person you have ever met, and every person you will ever meet, has known pain and hardship. We wonder if our lives matter. We struggle with difficult decisions. We lose people we love. Life isn't easy. If the Bible could not speak into these circumstances, no one would read it, regardless of any theory of inspiration. Scripture teaches us the sustaining faith passed down to us by saints and martyrs. It shows us the way to a deeper, more meaningful life in the here and now, and leads us into eternal life with God. It makes us wise for salvation and equips us to do work that is about more than ourselves.

Theories of inspiration can be useful because they provide us with guidelines and help us to understand how and why God has spoken to us. They also compel us to engage passages of Scripture that we might otherwise ignore. Yet in adopting one theory or another, we should remember that the meaningfulness of Scripture does not depend on a particular understanding of inspiration. It depends upon God. God is alive, and God reaches out to us in and through the words of the Bible. Therefore, we search the Scriptures. We pray over them. We listen to them in worship. We sing their words. Ultimately, we are formed by God's work through them into the people we are meant to be. We have become participants in the divine nature.

The Authority of the Bible

Along with the inspiration of the Bible, we sometimes speak of the *authority* of the Bible. This is an important matter, and it is difficult to get right. In some traditions, the concept of the authority of Scripture has been almost entirely lost. The time in which we live is highly individualistic and quite often anti-authoritarian. Thus the idea of a book that has *authority* over our lives is deeply countercultural. As we think about the authority of Scripture, we should bear in mind that Scripture only has authority because of the authority of the God who stands behind it. Scripture's authority is "derived authority."[18] As N. T. Wright stated, the phrase "'authority of scripture,' when unpacked, offers a picture of God's sovereign and saving plan for the entire cosmos, dramatically inaugurated by Jesus himself, and now to be implemented through the Spirit-led life of the church *precisely as the scripture-reading community.*"[19]

Two Meanings of Authority

When we talk about authority, we usually mean a couple of different things. If someone has authority, he or she has been invested with a certain level of decision-making power and responsibility. To say that a professor has authority over her students is to speak of her prerogative to assign readings, evaluate papers, assign grades, shape course content, and direct classroom discussion. She has been invested with this authority by a larger institution with its own authority, such as a university.

Ideally, a person with authority has the qualifications to make the decisions for which he or she has responsibility. This leads to a second way in which we think about authority. If we say that this same professor speaks with authority on a particular topic, we mean that she is knowledgeable and competent regarding that topic. She *has* authority over the students, and she *speaks with* authority on the topics of her lectures.

By extension, when we talk about the authority of Scripture, we mean the extent to which Scripture makes binding claims on our lives. The Bible can make these binding claims because we believe that the power that stands behind it (like the university behind the professor) is the power of God. Scripture's authority flows out of God's authority. Further, we believe that Scripture can speak *with* authority on a variety of topics. It is a valid source of teaching about God, human beings, and the world in which we live. The professor may speak with authority because of her natural intelligence and many years of study. The Bible speaks with authority because it is God-breathed. It can teach us about God because it is from God. It can teach us about life because it is from the source of life. It can teach us about human relationships because it is from the one who lives eternally in a relationship of perfect love, the Holy Trinity. Scripture is binding upon our lives, and it can speak powerfully into the circumstances of our lives.

It is helpful to think about the authority of Scripture—God's authority—as something like that of a loving parent. A loving father or mother will place limits on what his or her children can do. A loving parent will offer advice, reproof, and counsel. A loving parent will even punish at times. By each of these actions, the parent means only to act in the best interest of the child, to teach the child wisdom, to help him or her avoid certain mistakes and adopt attitudes and patterns of behavior that will lead to the good life. Likewise, God wishes us to live a life that is truly good, which means being taken into the loving relationship of the Father, Son, and Holy Spirit. By understanding ourselves as standing under the loving authority of Scripture, we allow ourselves to be drawn ever more deeply into that loving relationship.

Difficulties with Biblical Authority

There are, however, some thorny issues related to the authority of Scripture. For example, there are passages in the Bible that condone slavery, silence women in church, and condone acts of shocking violence. In focusing on the goodness of Scripture, we should not simply set aside or ignore those passages of the Bible that seem distasteful or morally unacceptable to us. Instead, these texts need careful study and investigation in order to understand their function, especially as they relate to the broader witness of Scripture. As Kenton Sparks noted, from the time of the early church, "Christians struggled with the Bible's ethical diversity."[20] Thoughtful and faithful readers have developed a variety of strategies over the centuries for dealing with these difficult passages. We will look more closely at matters like these in chapter 5. For now, though, it is important to bear in mind that living under the authority of Scripture does not mean that every passage of Scripture is equally valuable for us or equally prescriptive. *The authority of the Bible is meant only to lead us ever more deeply into the life of God.* Keeping this in mind will help us as we engage the whole canon of Scripture.

Conclusion

People have used the Bible for many reasons over the centuries. The Bible can be gloriously illuminating or, when misused, painfully debilitating. As one pastor friend of mine said, the Bible in the hands of the wrong person can be like a loaded shotgun in the hands of a child. It is imperative, then, that we keep in mind that Scripture has been given to us for our good. Its purpose is to build us up in the life of faith and draw us closer to God. The Father, Son, and Holy Spirit exist eternally in a communion of perfect love, and God invites us into that blessed communion. Throughout our lives, we have the opportunity to commune with God more fully and, thereby, to be changed. Paul teaches us that if anyone is in Christ, there is a new creation (2 Corinthians 5:17). God created us, and God is re-creating us, molding us back into the people we were meant to be before sin distorted the divine image within us. Thus, as John Wesley once wrote, "[H]ow much soever any man hath attained, or in how high a degree soever he is perfect, he hath still need to 'grow in grace,' and daily to advance in the knowledge and love of God his Saviour."[21] Put in more modern language, no matter how much we grow in our faith and love of God, we can still grow more. God never stops inviting us to journey more deeply into the divine life. God's love is an inexhaustible fountain, and one of the most important ways in which we drink from this fountain is by our encounter with Scripture.

To say that Scripture is inspired is to say that God has guided the formation of the Bible at every level in order to draw us more deeply into the divine life. While theories of inspiration can be helpful, for most people they aren't particularly important. Rather, people tend to trust in Scripture because it guides them, encourages them, provides correction for them when they make mistakes, and gives them hope. In this sense, Scripture is authoritative. It speaks with wisdom and insight into the circumstances of our lives because of the wisdom and insight of the God who inspired it. God's authority over our lives is in many ways like that of a loving parent, and the primary resource we have for God's parental guidance is Scripture.

CHAPTER 1 STUDY QUESTIONS

1. How does the study of Scripture draw you closer to God's heart?

2. What difference does it make that Scripture is God-breathed/inspired?

3. What makes the inspiration of Scripture different from the inspiration that we receive today from God?

4. When has the Bible sustained you? In other words, how has the Bible spoken into your life circumstances?

5. Do you find yourself troubled by the authority of Scripture? If so, how might it become a loving authority under the loving relationship of God?

CHAPTER 2

READING FOR THE LIFE OF GOD

Years ago I met a remarkable man named Dean Drayton. I was a graduate student, and at the time he was the president-elect of the Uniting Church of Australia and a visiting professor at Perkins School of Theology. While he was teaching at Perkins I had the great pleasure of getting to know him a bit and to learn a great deal from him in the process. During some of our conversations, I noticed that when he spoke about God, he often spoke specifically of the "living God." I wondered why he chose to speak about God in this particular way. There are innumerable ways to describe God. We might speak of the "loving God," "God Almighty," or the "eternal God." I have a friend who always prays to "God in heaven." Many people refer to God as "Father," and still others will speak of the "creator God."

Dr. Drayton, however, chose to speak of the "living God." As I listened to him speak about God, it became clear to me why he did so. Through the course of his life, he had encountered God several times in deeply personal, powerful ways. These encounters with God changed him. They changed his heart. They changed his theology. As a result, they changed the way in which he talked about God. He knew God as "living," and that made all the difference for him.

You and I can also encounter the living God, and one of the most powerful resources we have for doing so is Scripture. We don't read the Bible just to learn *about* God. We also read the Bible to *get to know* God in a deeply personal way. Getting to know God is rather like getting to know a person. When you get to know someone, that person becomes a part of your life, and you become a part of his or her life. When you get to know God, you enter into the divine life, and God enters into your life. Scripture is a place where God and humans meet. If we seek God in the pages of Scripture, God will meet us there. As stated in the introduction to this book, the Bible is not just a resource for *information*, but also for *transformation*.

Through the centuries, Christians have developed ways of engaging Scripture for growth in the knowledge and love of God. In this chapter, we will look at a few of these, including prayer, meditation, and worship. This is certainly not an exhaustive list, but simply an overview of some of the church's ancient wisdom regarding the reading of Scripture for the life of faith.

Praying over the Bible

It is important to invite God into your reading of Scripture. There are many ways to do this. Sometimes, just a simple prayer will do: "God, guide my thoughts and fill my heart through this reading. Help me become the person you want me to be." Sometimes you may wish to read Scripture before or after an extended period of prayer. Perhaps you wish to have a period of silent prayer, inviting God to speak to you and guide you as you quiet your heart in preparation for your reading. Or, you may wish to use one of the ancient prayers of the church, such as the following from the fourth-century theologian John Chrysostom:

> O Lord Jesus Christ, open Thou the eyes of my heart, that I may hear Thy word and understand and do Thy will, for I am a sojourner upon the earth. Hide not Thy commandments from me, but open mine eyes, that I may perceive the wonders of Thy law. Speak unto me the hidden and secret things of Thy wisdom. On Thee do I set my hope, O my God, that Thou shalt enlighten my mind and understanding with the light of Thy knowledge, not only to cherish those things which are written, but to do them; that in reading the lives and sayings of the saints I may not sin, but that such may serve for my restoration, enlightenment and sanctification, for the salvation of my soul, and the inheritance of life everlasting. For Thou art the enlightenment of those who lie in darkness, and from Thee cometh every good deed and every gift. Amen.[1]

The language of this prayer may seem old and outdated, but the ideas it expresses are powerful. That is often the case with prayers that have been preserved and handed down through the centuries. People have preserved them because they speak to common desires and experiences of human life, and I encourage you to work your way through this prayer slowly. Think about what you are praying and offer the words up to God.

However we pray, it is important that we *do* pray. It is absolutely crucial that *God* is at work in us as we encounter the Bible. God must prepare our hearts, plant the seeds of wisdom in us as we read, and nurture the growth of our faith by the power of the Holy Spirit after we read. John Wesley spoke of how crucial it is to end a time of reading Scripture with prayer, "that what we read may be written on our hearts."[2] Our reading should be steeped in prayer because we hope that, through our reading, God will change us, restoring within us the image of God that has been tarnished by sin.

Another way of putting this is to say that we need for God to provide us with illumination when we read the Bible. In her book *God the Spirit*, Beth Felker Jones wrote that the term *illumination* refers to "the way in which the Spirit continues to work in and with God's people, as readers of Scripture, to help us understand and be faithful to what we read there."[3] The term *inspiration*, she says, refers to God's work in and through the biblical writers in the past. Inspiration and illumination, then, come from the same source, but they serve different purposes. God inspired the biblical writers to create works that would guide first Israel and then the church. God illuminates our readings so that we can grasp more deeply the meaning of the inspired writings.[4] God might give us insights when we read books other than the Bible as well, but it is not the same because these other works are not inspired in the same way as the Bible. The Bible is *uniquely* inspired to guide us as people of faith, and the illuminating power of the Holy Spirit leads us through the Scriptures and more deeply into the life of God.[5]

Biblical scholar Daniel Patte described an experience in Botswana in which he encountered a form of communal preaching. "A woman from the congregation stood up, read [the Scripture passage], and preached. Others followed her lead, as they felt moved by the Spirit." At the end of each of these mini-sermons, the preacher would say, "Brothers and sisters pray for me, so that I might better understand the Scripture."[6] The members of the congregation would then fall on their knees together, praying aloud. These African Christians understood that God is a living, active presence in our midst, and that God's guidance is necessary if we are to read and hear the Bible in ways that will help us to grow in the life of faith. They pray not only for their own understanding, but for the understanding of others in the community. This is a helpful corrective for many of us in the West. The work of God is both individual and communal, and our prayers over the Bible should be not simply for ourselves, but for others whom we call brothers and sisters in Christ.

In fact, apart from the guidance of the Holy Spirit, we cannot read Scripture properly, either as individuals or as a community. The Bible lends itself to many different interpretations, and while there may not be one right interpretation of a particular passage, there are many wrong ones. We depend upon the guidance of the Spirit so that the reading of the Bible may result in the "renewing of [our] minds" (Rom. 12:2). When we pray in faith, the Holy Spirit prays within us through the Son to the Father. We are guided by God in our prayers, and God will teach us what to look for, listen for, and seek out in our reading of the Bible. God will enliven our minds and clear our thoughts in such a way that the Bible can speak words of renewed life to us.

Praying with the Bible

It is crucial to pray *over* the text before, during, and after our reading. Yet some passages of the Bible also lend themselves to the practice of praying *with* the text. In other words, the words of Scripture can become our prayer. This practice is especially common with the Psalms. Take, for example, the first two verses of Psalm 51:

> Have mercy on me, O God,
>> according to your unfailing love;
> according to your great compassion
>> blot out my transgressions.
> Wash away all my iniquity
>> and cleanse me from my sin.

Here is a prayer of repentance. Each of us sins. As the Spirit works in our heart, we feel remorse over our sins. We have acted against God and other people, and we need to feel God's forgiveness. Therefore we might offer up the beginning of this psalm as a prayer. We want God's mercy. We rely on his unfailing love and great compassion. Only God can blot out our transgressions, wash away our iniquities, and cleanse us from sin. Therefore, we offer up this prayer in repentance and humility, and at the same time receive God's mercy and forgiveness available to us through Jesus Christ. We might feel a palpable sense of relief. We might feel God's love flowing through us. Or, while we might not have a powerful sense of God's working in that moment, we will know that we have confessed our sins before God, we are hiding nothing, and we are promised through the gospel that we are forgiven.

There might be times in our lives when we are so filled with gratitude that we wish to sing praises to God, but our own words may seem inadequate. In those cases, we may wish to pray aloud one of the psalms of praise, such as Psalm 46:

> God is our refuge and strength,
>> an ever-present help in trouble.
> Therefore we will not fear, though the earth give way
>> and the mountains fall into the heart of the sea,
> though its waters roar and foam
>> and the mountains quake with their surging. . . .
> He says, "Be still, and know that I am God;
>> I will be exalted among the nations,
>> I will be exalted in the earth."
> The LORD Almighty is with us;
>> the God of Jacob is our fortress. (vv. 1–3, 10–11)

By contrast, for each of us, there are times when we are in great distress. Life can be hard, painful, almost unbearable at times. It is simply a part of the Christian life that there are seasons when God seems distant, even absent. Psalm 22 can help us to give voice to these feelings in prayer, just as it did for Jesus as he hung upon the cross:

> My God, my God, why have you forsaken me?
>> Why are you so far from saving me,
>> so far from my cries of anguish?
> My God, I cry out by day, but you do not answer,
>> by night, but I find no rest. (vv. 1–2)

These kinds of feelings have always been around, and they always will be. They are a normal part of the life of faith, and their scriptural expressions are available to us as we seek God in prayer.

Meditating upon the Text

Another way of inviting God to renew our hearts and minds is through meditation upon Scripture. Richard Foster wrote, "What happens in meditation is that we create the emotional and spiritual space which allows Christ to construct an inner sanctuary in the heart."[7] When we meditate on Scripture, we remove ourselves from the many distractions in life which can be roadblocks to God's work in our hearts. In our engagement with Scripture, we often focus on tools of the trade, like biblical history and word studies. The meditation on Scripture, says Foster, is a different approach. It "centers on internalizing and personalizing the passage. The written Word becomes a living word addressed to you."[8]

Meditation is very difficult for most people. It takes practice and discipline. Our minds are prone to wander. This is particularly true in the context of the modern West in which we are constantly exposed to so many different stimuli. We are used to things moving at a fast pace and having instant access to information. Between television, the Internet, and cell phones, we have to be intentional if we are ever to have a moment of peace and quiet. If you try meditating on Scripture and find you are having difficulty concentrating, don't give up. With some effort, you can develop the skills of meditation and consciously focus your mind on words of Scripture. You will surely find it a rewarding practice if you do.

There is not one right way to meditate upon Scripture. By experimenting with different kinds of meditation, you will find out which ones work for you. In the medieval church, meditation often involved memorization of Scripture, and at times the passages that were memorized were quite long. It was normally monks who engaged in this practice, since they had both access to the sacred texts and time to memorize them.[9] The monks would memorize portions of the Bible and recite them throughout the day as they went about their various tasks. The recitation was done out loud, not just in the mind. This oral recitation was considered a form of reading. It was, moreover, considered a form of prayer. As they read aloud, the words of Scripture became their prayers.[10]

We live in a very different context than the medieval monks, however, one in which printed books are more readily available. We can find just about whatever we want on the Internet, and our skills of memorization are generally not as well-developed as those who lived in earlier times. Therefore, it might be better to begin with the memorization of a short passage of Scripture that you could recite throughout the day. Take, for example, 2 Timothy 1:7: "the Spirit God gave us does not make us timid, but gives us power, love and self-discipline." You may wish to recite this passage again and again, letting its meaning sink in more fully with each repetition. Or you may wish to recite it slowly, and think about different aspects of this short passage. God gave us the Spirit, and this Spirit does not make us timid. What does this mean to you? How would life look in a spirit of timidity? Is this how you live your life? The Spirit gives us power, but what kind of power? The Spirit gives us love. Does this mean that we receive love from God, or that we are given the ability to love others, or both? How do you see this in your life? The Spirit gives us self-discipline. In what parts of our lives do we need greater self-discipline? What would that look like for us?

You need not memorize a passage, though, to meditate upon it. Let's look at the description of Christ that is given in Revelation 1:13–18. As John of Patmos describes Christ, he is:

> dressed in a robe reaching down to his feet and with a golden sash around his chest. The hair on his head was white like wool, as white as snow, and his eyes were like blazing fire. His feet were like bronze glowing in a furnace, and his voice was like the sound of rushing waters. In his right hand he held seven stars, and coming out of his mouth was a sharp, double-edged sword. His face was like the sun shining in all its brilliance.
>
> When I saw him, I fell at his feet as though dead. Then he placed his right hand on me and said: "Do not be afraid. I am the First and the Last. I am the Living One; I was dead, and now look, I am alive for ever and ever! And I hold the keys of death and Hades."

If you slowly make your way down through this passage, images of Christ will form in your mind: his robe and golden sash, his white hair and blazing eyes, his feet like bronze, glowing with heat. You may imagine Christ's voice like rushing water. Other images may be equally powerful. Can you envision the seven stars in his right hand and the sword coming forth from his mouth? Is it any wonder that John falls down as though dead?

Yet despite this overwhelming presence, Christ commands, "Do not be afraid." It seems like a rather tall order, but there is a reason for the audacity of this instruction: Christ was dead, but now he is alive, and he will never die again. He holds the keys to death and Hades. This is worth spending some time on. Jesus has conquered death, which lies at the root of so much human fear and the actions that spring forth from that fear. Jesus has overcome the condemnation that human beings have brought upon themselves by their sin. Rather than death and Hades, Christ offers us eternal life with him. Christ owns the past, present, and future, and if he is our Lord, we need fear neither death nor condemnation.

It is one thing to read this passage of Scripture, but another to live in the light of its truth. We don't just want to read Scripture. We want to internalize it. We want its words to course through our lives. We want it to nourish our spiritual lives the way food and water nourish our bodies. We are inadvertently formed as people by so many different sources: advertising, the Internet, education, our peer groups, our upbringing. In the present culture of the modern West, we must be extremely intentional if we want to be formed by Scripture. It is not simply something that occurs by happenstance. We do not hear verses from the Bible every time we turn on the television. Most of the time the ads that pop up on websites do not contain Bible verses, and even if they do we probably don't pay much attention to them. Meditation on the text allows us to receive God's words to us at a deep level. It is a way of keeping a steady pace on the pathway into the life of God, and a time-honored practice that has borne much fruit in the history of our faith.

Lectio Divina

Over the centuries, Christians have developed many different ways of engaging the Bible. One time-honored practice that dates back to the middle ages is called *lectio divina*, which roughly translates as "divine reading." Lectio divina is a method that combines meditation and prayer. There is not simply one way to practice lectio divina. There are many books and websites that can help you develop this practice. What follows is a basic outline that those who practice lectio divina often use.

The first step is to find a quiet place where you can engage in prayer and meditation. For many of us, finding a quiet place can be very difficult. Life moves along quickly. We have alarms on our phone that notify us of appointments. We receive messages via text and social media. We have to get the kids to school, sports, or church. We have to get to work on time. We have work to do when we get home. We rush through our days.

Lectio divina is the opposite of this. It is an unrushed, quiet activity, and it requires unrushed time and a quiet space. A coffee shop with music in the background, people coming in and out, and conversations going on around you is probably not the best place. You may have to think for awhile to find quiet space and time. Turn off your cell phone. Close your laptop. God often speaks to us in silence. The clutter of our lives can obscure God's gentle voice.

Identify a passage of the Bible you want to read. A good way to start is by using one of the Psalms or a passage from the Gospels. Read slowly through the text. It may be helpful to read out loud. Listen to the sounds of the words as you read them. As you work your way through the text, some word or phrase may stand out so meaningfully to you that you wish to stop and stay there. You have thus found the centerpiece of your meditation. If this does not happen every time, you should not be concerned. Lectio divina is not a task-oriented activity. It is a way of resting in God's Word, allowing the Holy Spirit to guide you

Once you have read through the text—or at least as far as you feel led to read—guide your mind toward meditation on the text. Did certain words jump out at you? What images are left in your mind? What feelings did this text evoke within you? If there is a particular phrase that you found meaningful, begin to repeat it by memory—again, slowly. Stay with the place or places in your reading that stood out for you. You may be surprised at which words or phrases catch your attention. This is a good thing. It is the Spirit leading you in unexpected directions. There is no set time period for which you must meditate. Move in the Spirit as feels right to you.

Gradually your meditation will become prayer. Whatever you have received from God in your meditation, offer back up to God in prayer. This is your response to God's gift to you in your meditation. Be open to the leadings of the Spirit as you pray. You may find that God leads you to silent prayer. You don't always need to speak, either out loud or in your mind, as you pray. Sometimes it is best simply to remain in silence and wait for the Spirit to guide your thoughts and words.

Finally, simply rest in the Spirit. This is a time just for listening. Is God saying anything in particular to you? Is God working on some area of your life? Sit with God in silence for a time. Allow God to shape your heart through your meditation and prayer.

There is no single method of encountering the Bible that works equally well for everyone. People are wired differently from one another. We have different natural predispositions, and we've been formed by the world around us in different ways. Nevertheless, it is often helpful for us to look to those who came before us in the faith and learn from the time-honored practices that have sustained

Christians through the centuries. Lectio divina is one such practice that has guided many believers in their journey into the life of God.

The Bible in Corporate Worship

We don't just encounter the Bible in the power of the Spirit in our private devotional lives, but in corporate worship as well. In fact, this is where most Christians have encountered the Bible throughout Christian history. In the ancient world in which the writings of the Bible emerged, most people could not read. Those who could read usually did so out loud. Silent, private reading would not become commonplace until later in history. A member of the community would read passages of Scripture—even whole books of the Bible—out loud to those who were gathered. The second-century Christian Justin Martyr wrote that, when Christians gathered for worship, they would read from the Gospels [the "memoirs of the Apostles"] or prophets for as long as time would permit.[11] This would likely be the only time that many of these believers had access to their sacred writings. Additionally, books were very expensive in the ancient world. Remember that the printing press wasn't invented until the fifteenth century. Books had to be copied by hand, which was a long, laborious, and expensive process. The Christian Bible found its first uses in worship, and the best worship today will continue to emphasize the communal encounter with Scripture.

Lectionaries and Sermon Series

Some churches follow the lectionary, a list of weekly texts used by congregations around the world. There are a few texts chosen for each week, and the worship service is built around some of these texts. An advantage of the lectionary is that it leads preachers to engage and proclaim parts of the Bible they might otherwise ignore. In the same way, it prevents preachers from focusing too often on their favorite texts. The use of the lectionary, however, is not always easy. It is a discipline. More than once when I have used it I've questioned my decision: *I have to preach on one of these texts?* My experience, though, is that deep engagement with texts we might otherwise pass over can yield treasures of insight. The wisdom available within a given passage of Scripture is not always apparent at first blush.

By contrast, many churches today use thematic sermon series rather than the lectionary. In other words, the sermons for several consecutive weeks will be on a particular theme, such as "How to Deal with Anger," or "The Christian Marriage." This practice can be helpful as well, but there is also a danger here. The text can become the servant of the series theme, and its meaning can be lost in the attempt to craft a relevant message. A good sermon is a reflection upon the teachings of the Bible. There are many ways to do this, many different styles and practices of preaching, but regardless of how one preaches, *the preacher must let the Bible speak.* A passage of Scripture has its own voice, to be lifted up and drawn out by the preacher's voice. Yes, it is good to hear the words of Scripture read aloud in worship, but if the main reason for using Scripture is to support our "Really Big Idea" for the week, we are not actually engaging the text. Instead we are leveraging the authority of the Bible in support of our own agendas. All this being said, it doesn't take a sermon series for a preacher to obscure the voice of the text with his or her own voice, and a sermon series can provide opportunities for serious and faithful engagement with Scripture.

When we read the Bible aloud in worship, we sometimes say things like, "The Word of God for the people of God," or "May the

Lord add his blessing to the reading of his Holy Word." The first of these is a declaration of the centrality of Scripture in the Christian life. The second is a prayer, an invocation of the Spirit to guide us as we encounter the words of the Bible. It is crucial that we acknowledge and invoke the work of God as we receive the Word of God. Do we ever hear the words of the Bible read dispassionately, as if by rote, in our worship services? It is easy to take for granted the great gift that God has given us through the church in Scripture. It is also easy to go through the motions of worship without truly acknowledging the Spirit of God in our midst. But think about what the reading of Scripture in worship is: we are speaking the divinely inspired words given by God to the church for our salvation, and we are asking the very same God to bless our hearing, renew our minds, and transform our wills. That is no small thing! Acknowledging the presence of the living God as we read Scripture helps us perceive both the gravity and potential of our reading.

Scripture in Song

One of the most powerful ways to encounter the words of the Bible in worship is through song. It is no wonder that Jewish and Christian traditions have preserved an entire book of songs, or, as they are called, psalms. From the earliest days of the church, Christians have sung their faith. Scripture itself teaches us of the value of singing. We are instructed in Ephesians, "be filled with the Spirit, speaking to one another with psalms, hymns, and songs from the Spirit. Sing and make music from your heart to the Lord, always giving thanks to God the Father for everything, in the name of our Lord Jesus Christ" (5:18–20). Likewise, Colossians teaches us, "Let the message of Christ dwell among you richly as you teach and admonish one another with all wisdom through psalms, hymns, and songs from the Spirit, singing to God with gratitude in your hearts" (3:16). A wise saying from the early church, often attributed to Augustine, is, "The one who sings prays twice."

As many a churchgoer can attest, our music in worship varies in its fidelity to Scripture. Though some songs seem only superficially acquainted to the biblical witness, others provide deep and meaningful reflections on biblical themes. Think of the hymn, "Holy, Holy, Holy! Lord God Almighty!" written by Reginald Heber. The second verse of this hymn goes:

> Holy, Holy, Holy! all the saints adore Thee,
> Casting down their golden crowns around the glassy sea;
> Cherubim and Seraphim falling down before Thee,
> Which wert, and art, and evermore shalt be.[12]

This is a depiction of the scene from Revelation 4:6–11, in which four "living creatures" sing of God's holiness day and night. And as they sing, twenty-four elders fall down before the throne and worship God. They fall on their faces and cast their crowns down before God in a posture of eternal worship. And they sing of God's worthiness to receive glory, honor, and power because it is through God that all things came into being.

Some songs, moreover, are adaptations of the very words of Scripture. One popular song of the church is called "This Is the Day" by Les Garrett. The first verse is adapted straight from Psalm 118:24. (Check the translation in the New King James Version rather than the NIV for a closer equivalence.)

> This is the day, this is the day
> that the Lord has made, that the Lord has made;
> we will rejoice, we will rejoice
> and be glad in it, and be glad in it.

This is the day that the Lord has made;

we will rejoice and be glad in it.

This is the day, this is the day that the Lord has made.[13]

Or consider these lines from the popular worship song, "Everlasting God":

You are the everlasting God

The everlasting God

You do not faint

You won't grow weary

You're the defender of the weak

You comfort those in need

You lift us up on wings like eagles[14]

These lyrics are simply an adaptation of Isaiah 40, especially verses 28–31.

When we sing our Scriptures, not only do we offer praise to God, but we learn the words of Scripture and internalize its themes, thereby opening our hearts and minds to formation by these inspired and holy texts.

Holy Communion

The rite of Holy Communion (also called the Lord's Supper and the Eucharist) is another way in which we encounter Scripture in the context of worship. The various Christian traditions often practice Communion quite differently from one another. They understand it differently as well. Some see Communion as a remembrance of Christ's Last Supper and sacrifice on our behalf. Some see it as a means of grace, a reliable way of receiving the work of the Holy Spirit for the purification of our hearts. Some traditions hold that

Christ really is present—but spiritually so—in the bread and wine (or juice). The Roman Catholic and Eastern Orthodox traditions teach that the bread and wine undergo transubstantiation, meaning that the bread and wine really change into the body and blood of Christ.

Regardless of these differences, in most traditions, during the rite of Communion there is a recitation of the scriptural story of salvation, followed by a recitation of the words of institution, those words that Christ said to his disciples during his Last Supper with them. For example, take this passage from the Great Thanksgiving, a rite of Communion in the *Book of Common Prayer*:

> We give thanks to you, O God, for the goodness and love which you have made known to us in creation; in the calling of Israel to be your people; in your Word spoken through the prophets; and above all in the Word made flesh, Jesus, your Son. For in these last days you sent him to be incarnate from the Virgin Mary, to be the Savior and Redeemer of the world. In him, you have delivered us from evil, and made us worthy to stand before you. In him, you have brought us out of error into truth, out of sin into righteousness, out of death into life.[15]

This is not a quotation from any one part of the Bible, but a brief summary of the Bible's story of salvation. It is scriptural in the sense that all of it is derived from Scripture. It is a way of directing us back into Scripture in order to understand and receive the salvation that God offers to us. These mighty acts of God are for the salvation of human beings, and they culminate in Christ's death and resurrection.

Usually after the Great Thanksgiving, we recite the words of institution. In other words, we recount what Christ said to his disciples: "Take, eat: This is my Body, which is given for you. Do this for the remembrance of me," and "Drink this, all of you: This is my Blood of the New Covenant, which is shed for you and for many for the forgiveness of sins. Whenever you drink it, do this for the remembrance of me."[16] While various renderings of these words appear in Matthew 26:26–28, Mark 14:22–24, and Luke 22:17–20, the version used here, and in other versions of the Communion service, resembles 1 Corinthians 11:23–25 most closely. What we have, however, is a summary of the words of Scripture recounting Jesus' instructions to his disciples, not a direct quotation from any particular passage of Scripture. This is followed by a recitation of the Lord's Prayer, an adaptation of Matthew 6:9–13. After praying, the gathered body of Christ acts out the instruction that Christ gave to his disciples as they receive the bread and the cup.

Not all traditions have specific rites of Holy Communion, but among those that do, this ritual provides a powerful way of internalizing Scripture's broad narrative of salvation and recounting what Jesus taught his disciples about the way in which they should remember him. It is a way of receiving all over again God's saving work on our behalf, and thereby moving more deeply into God's divine life. Kenneth Loyer put the matter this way: "By God's grace the bread and the cup become for us symbols that convey, far more powerfully than mere pictures ever could, a living reality that is Christ's presence with us."[17]

Conclusion

We don't simply read the Bible for *information*. We read the Bible for *transformation*. We don't just want to know *about* God. We want to *know* God. And so we pray, we meditate, we sing, we imagine, we worship, and we wait for God to speak to us through the Bible. One way to engage the Bible is simply to sit down and begin reading; to study its words, stories, poems, and ideas; take notes; and apprehend what we encounter with the analytical part of our minds. This type of study is important, but it is not enough. If we really want to move within God's divine life, if we want to read with the aim of being changed by God, then we should engage the creative parts of our minds, the loving parts, the aspects of our beings in which we experience joy, sorrow, and gratitude.

Reading, singing, and reciting the words of the Bible in our worship are ways of confessing our faith together. It has what theologians call a catechetical function. A catechesis is a process whereby Christians learn the truths of the faith. Some traditions, such as the Roman Catholic Church, have a very formal process of catechesis. Other traditions may be less formal, though no less invested in teaching what they believe. Regardless, the Scriptures we read together, the sermons we receive, the songs we sing, and the rituals we perform shape our faith. They shape not only our intellect, but our hearts, our wills, and volitions. We should take seriously the fact that in our worship, we are not simply honoring God (though this is very important), but being *formed* as Christians.

Christian formation, however, is not simply a matter of internalizing the words of the Bible. For true formation to happen, we must encounter Christ ever more deeply through the power of the Holy Spirit. We must enter more fully into the life of God. As Christians we believe that God *really is present* in our worship. Christ promises us in Matthew 18:20, "Where two or three gather in my name, there am I with them." In worship, Christ is in our midst. The words of Scripture read aloud, preached, sung, and recited serve as a pathway into the life of God. The Spirit takes us by the hand and leads us down this pathway as we honor Christ together.

CHAPTER 2 STUDY QUESTIONS

1. What is the difference between knowing about God and knowing God personally?

2. Do you currently invite God into your reading of Scripture? If not, take time before your next encounter with Scripture and invite God into it.

3. What is the difference between illumination and inspiration?

4. Have you ever prayed with Scripture or used words of Scripture for your prayers? Take this opportunity to pray using one of the psalms provided in the "Praying with the Bible" section or another passage of Scripture that presently speaks to your heart and/or situation.

5. How is meditating on Scripture different from just reading it? Why is it important to meditate on Scripture?

CHAPTER 3

GUIDES INTO THE LIFE OF GOD

Sometimes you hear things that stick with you, but you don't know why. That happened to me once when I heard the theologian Frances Young speaking about Paul's letter to the Philippians. In 2:5–11, Paul quoted a song that the early Christians sang together. He did this to remind these Christians that their thoughts, words, and deeds should be modeled on those of Jesus.

> In your relationships with one another, have the same mindset as Christ Jesus:
>
> Who, being in very nature God, did not consider equality with God something to be used to his own advantage; rather, he made himself nothing by taking the very nature of a servant, being made in human likeness. And being found in appearance as a man, he humbled himself by becoming obedient to death— even death on a cross! Therefore God exalted him to the highest place and gave him the name that is above every name, that at the name of Jesus every knee should bow, in heaven and on earth and under the earth, and every tongue acknowledge that Jesus Christ is Lord, to the glory of God the Father.

Young was reflecting on this passage in reference to the life of her adult son, Arthur, who was born with severe intellectual disabilities. "In the Incarnation," she said, "God takes on human weakness." When God became a human being in Jesus Christ, he became vulnerable to all the things to which each of us is vulnerable. Christ had all power, all honor and authority, and gave this up for people like you and me. He had the nature of God, but he voluntarily took on the nature of a servant. Therefore, people like Arthur, so vulnerable, so weak by the standards of the wider culture, show us qualities of human life that Christ voluntarily took upon himself. When we encounter Arthur, we see something of God that we may have missed before.

Sometimes you hear things that stick with you, but you don't know why . . . though you may learn later. In 2006 I was in the neonatal ward of a hospital in Dayton, Ohio. I had just learned that my son Sean had Down syndrome. For my wife and me, this was some of the hardest news we have ever had to hear. Along with our older son, Luke, we have been on a journey with Sean for years now that has taught us about faith, patience, strength, weakness, compassion, suffering, and joy. But from the first moments of Sean's diagnosis, I have been helped by thinking through Young's reflections on Christ and her own son. Like Arthur, there are things that Sean teaches us that we would not learn otherwise. Sean has drawn us more deeply into the life of God, and Young's reflections on the song of Philippians 2 offered a very important guidepost along the way.

In the incarnation, God takes on human weakness. I have been ruminating on that idea for more than a decade. I'm not sure I would have come to frame the issue this way if I had not heard Young speaking on that day. Her words, however, have helped me to make theological sense out of my own son's life as a person with a disability. Here is an example of the way in which the community of faith has helped me personally to interpret the Bible. Young is a Christian, speaking and writing for Christians, and I am a Christian receiving her wisdom born of experience, reflection on the Bible, and prayer. In this way, engagement with the community of believers has proved to be extremely important for my development in the life of faith.

Christians and Community

Many Christians today practice a deeply individualistic form of faith. Faith is personal. It is about my relationship with Jesus Christ. It is about my personal salvation and my personal walk with God. Indeed, these descriptions of Christianity are true. The Christian faith is a personal faith. It affects the way a person thinks, speaks, and acts. It involves a relationship of love between a man or woman and the eternal God. While these descriptions are true, however, they are also inadequate. Christian faith is personal, but it is not *only* personal. There is a communal aspect of the faith that is crucial to our participation in the life of God.

When we have questions about our faith or face tough moral problems, it is important that we consult the community of believers, both those with whom we share this earthly life and those of years, decades, and centuries past. The wisdom of the saints, both past and present, is one of the great treasures of the faith. When we are confused about matters of faith, we can seek help from others around us. When we face times of doubt, it is well for us to confide in and seek the wisdom of fellow travellers on this journey into the life of God. And when we read the Bible, we are helped by the insights, prayers, and wisdom of other believers.

Life in God's Household

Once you become a Christian, you are explicitly no longer your own. Of course, each of us belongs to God from the day we are born until the day we die. Becoming a Christian, however, is a public acknowledgment of this fact. We are God's, and by accepting Christ we become a part of God's household. There was a time when we were estranged from God, but now God has brought us near. As it says in Ephesians 2:19–22:

> Consequently, you are no longer foreigners and strangers, but fellow citizens with God's people and also members of his household, built on the foundation of the apostles and prophets, with Christ Jesus himself as the chief cornerstone. In him the whole building is joined together and rises to become a holy temple in the Lord. And in him you too are being built together to become a dwelling in which God lives by his Spirit.

Likewise, in 1 Peter 2:9–10 we read, "you are a chosen people, a royal priesthood, a holy nation, God's special possession, that you may declare the praises of him who called you out of darkness into his wonderful light. Once you were not a people, but now you are the people of God; once you had not received mercy, but now you have received mercy."

Once you were not a people, but now you are the people of God. You share a baptism. You share a faith. And you share the sacred Scriptures. The Bible is not simply yours or mine. It is *ours.* Thus, when we come to read the Bible, we come not simply as individuals, but as members of the household of God interpreting the Bible as it was meant to be interpreted: in community. Our faith was never meant to be a primarily individualistic affair. Jesus created a community of followers around himself. He left his closest followers to carry out his mission, and he sent the Holy Spirit to guide the church. Corporate worship and discernment have always been a part of the Christian life. Yes, time alone, say, in prayer or meditation, is indeed valuable, but it is equally important that we return to our community of faith.

There is another danger besides individualism, though. It is that our faith will be shaped by a community, but not primarily by the Christian community. Particularly in the United States, it is easy for us to confuse the values of the wider culture with the values of the church. Without realizing it, we may "baptize" cultural values and call them Christian. I have seen this happen within Christian traditions from the very liberal to the very conservative. I am sure that at times I have done this myself. Scripture teaches us, however, that sin has affected not only the way people behave, but the way in which we perceive right and wrong. Paul in particular told us not to be conformed to the world's way of thinking, but rather to be transformed by the renewing of our minds (Romans 12:2). Therefore, the way we think about every aspect of our lives must be given to God in prayer and examined by Scripture, within the community of faith, in light of the Christian tradition. Whether we are talking about the beginning and end of life, human sexuality, marriage and divorce, the care of the poor, the use of armed force, the status of refugees, or race relations, we should try to understand each of these matters in *specifically Christian* ways. Christians must necessarily see the world around them differently than other people. We cannot trust that the right answer to ethical problems will simply emerge in time out of the wider cultures in which we live.

Working out Our Faith Together

Paul instructed us to, "work out your salvation with fear and trembling" (Phil. 2:12). Indeed, this is good advice, because working out our salvation is no less than ordering our lives so as to be in right relationship with the God of the universe. That is no small thing. It shapes both our present lives and our eternal destinies. Thankfully, we don't have to do this on our own. In fact, we should not even try to do it on our own. If we read this passage in Greek we can see that the word "your" is plural. We don't have a plural form of "you" in English (except for "y'all"), so we may easily miss part of what Paul is saying here: the working out of our salvation is something we do together with other Christians, not something we do in isolation from one another. A document created by the World Council of Churches explained the issue very nicely: "The Church is not merely the sum of individual believers in communion with God, nor primarily the mutual communion of individual believers among themselves. *It is their common partaking in the life of God* (2 Pet. 1:4), who as Trinity is the source and focus of all communion."[1] Our journey into the life of God is one we are meant to take with other people.

Surely reading the Bible is a key element of our journey of faith. Yet as we travel along the pathway into the life of God, we will miss important landmarks, life-giving springs, beautiful scenery, and rest stops if we travel alone. The pathway, moreover, is not always clearly marked. The proper way to interpret the Bible is not always obvious to us, either as individuals or as a community. Therefore, we need the wisdom of our brothers and sisters in the faith to help us along, to keep us from heading down rabbit trails, into dead ends, or off of cliffs. Our individual interpretations do matter, but we should be ever mindful of the wisdom of other believers. The Bible is, in fact, a product of communal Christian reflection. We first chose Jewish writings, and produced our own writings, for use in worship and teaching—activities that require a community.[2] The very origins of the Bible are within the believing community.

Occasionally we hear stories of a person who picks up the Bible and begins reading, and in the process has a conversion experience and receives Christ into his or her heart. We give thanks when things like this happen, but we should bear in mind that these events are exceedingly rare. Almost all people are brought to faith through relationships—with parents, brothers and sisters, husbands and wives, and friends. If coming to faith is born of relationships, how much more is growth in the faith? Personally, I cannot name all the people who helped me to grow in the knowledge and love of God. I was raised in the faith, and my parents took care to know that I had a Christian formation as a child. Sunday school teachers, youth leaders, Christian friends, seminary professors, pastors, my colleagues in the seminary where I now serve—all of these people have shaped the ways in which I have come to know and love God. Growth in faith requires the support of a community. This is no less the case for reading and understanding Scripture than for any other part of the Christian life.

When I was a kid growing up in Texas, there were generally two things that we talked about when the extended family got together during holidays: football and faith, most often in that order. With regard to football, it was generally agreed that the Dallas Cowboys were God's favorite team (remember: this was Texas in the 1970s and 80s), though when the conversation turned to college football there was likely to be a wider divergence of opinions. When it came to faith, however, that was when the real discussion began. There were generally three main participants in this conversation: my Uncle Jim, Uncle Otis, and my dad. Uncle Jim was a United Methodist pastor (later United Church of Christ) who had been educated at Perkins, Claremont, and Vanderbilt. He was the very quintessence of a 1960s liberal. Uncle Otis was Jim's polar ideological opposite. He was former military, a housing contractor, and for church he alternated between Baptist and Pentecostal congregations. My dad, a United Methodist, was somewhere between the two, and he generally just liked to stir things up.

That the conversation would turn to religion was inevitable. Our lives were all deeply formed by the church, Scripture, and a Texas culture that still understood itself as Christian. You can probably guess that, whatever matter of Christian belief or practice they took up, these three characters rarely agreed on anything. They all had good reasons for the opinions they held, and they probably even changed one another's mind a bit (though none would ever admit it). For them it was all good fun, a way to pass the time after an afternoon meal. For me it was fascinating. I learned in these backyard seminars about the significance of conversation, of listening and discernment. My own ideas were being shaped and formed. I was learning in the long tradition of Christian communal reflection. My uncles and my dad wouldn't have called it that, but that is what it was.

Reading in community is an act of humility. None of us has all the answers. None of us is a perfect interpreter of the Bible. A particularly unique understanding of a passage of Scripture is not likely a very good one.[3] We are fellow travelers on the pathway into the life of God. The biblical scholar James Sanders wrote that we should consider ourselves to be pilgrims: "The model of the believing community . . . is that of a pilgrim folk en route through the ambiguities of present reality to the threshold of truth."[4] In this life, we simply will not reach our final destination. We won't know it all. We will never apprehend the whole truth about God. We will not fully understand all that God has done for us. For our entire Christian lives, we are moving more deeply into the life of God. But God is eternal and, therefore, there is always infinitely more to perceive, learn, and take in. We are pilgrims who know that our journey in this life will never end. Yet the journey itself is far richer than remaining at our original starting point ever could have been.

For Example . . . Evil Speaking

Let's take a concrete example of the way in which reading in community helps in the work of biblical interpretation. Matthew 5:21–22 raises at least two issues that should be of concern to most of us: anger and insult. In this passage, Jesus teaches, "You have heard that it was said to the people long ago, 'You shall not murder, and anyone who murders will be subject to judgment.' But I tell you that anyone who is angry with a brother or sister will be subject to judgment. Again, anyone who says to a brother or sister, 'Raca,' is answerable to the court. And anyone who says, 'You fool!' will be in danger of the fire of hell." Most of us will be able to prevent ourselves from committing murder, so on that count we're safe. But how many will be able to avoid becoming angry with another person? I would venture to say that not many of us are capable of this level of emotional control. So what are we to make of this passage? Is Jesus commanding us to do the impossible?

Consulting Scholars

One community that we might wish to consult is the scholarly community. The work of scholars who spend their professional lives in the academic study of the Bible can provide us with important resources as we engage our sacred texts. Biblical commentaries and Bible dictionaries, for example, can be very helpful for us as we try to understand the Bible. They can help us develop deeper understandings of the text. A few minutes with a Bible dictionary, for instance, can clarify the meaning of "Raca" in this passage. According to the *Eerdmans Dictionary of the Bible*, "raca" is "an expression of contempt," and is perhaps a transliteration of an Aramaic word, *rêqā*, which means "stupid fool."[5] Jesus, then, is admonishing his followers not to insult other people, and he reiterates this point in the next sentence: "And anyone who says 'You fool!' will be in danger of the fire of hell." The plain sense of the text teaches us that followers of Jesus must take care in how they speak to one another. To insult one another is a serious offense, serious enough that it should carry consequences among the community, and serious enough to make one liable to God's judgment.

One word of caution here: not all writings on the Bible are created equal. In the marketplace of ideas in which we live, there are as many interpretations as one can possibly imagine. If you can think of it, someone has probably written it. There is an incentive, moreover, for some publishers to put out work that says something new, different, appealing, or even shocking. Likewise, books that tell us what we want to hear will also sell. As 2 Timothy 4:3 teaches us, "the time will come when people will not put up with sound doctrine. Instead, to suit their own desires, they will gather around them a great number of teachers to say what their itching ears want to hear." It is very easy to find work that will be misleading and even harmful to the life of faith.

And this is not even to mention the Internet. In this day and age, anyone can publish virtually anything. This is a blessing and a curse. It is a blessing because it makes so much information freely available to so many people. It is a curse because so much of what one finds on the Internet is unreliable, irresponsible, and even downright sinful. When it comes to the Bible, the interpretive diversity one finds on the Internet is seemingly endless.

Additionally, the fact that someone goes by the title of "Reverend," "Pastor," "Bishop," or "Doctor" does not mean that he or she is a reliable interpreter of Scripture (or has even legitimately acquired those titles). The title before or the letters after a person's name do not necessarily mean that you should trust his or her judgment. As we read in 1 John 4:1, "do not believe every spirit, but test the spirits to see whether they are from God, because many false prophets have gone out into the world." The best way to find reliable written guides to the Bible is to consult with people whom you trust, whose lives demonstrate the fruit of the Spirit (Galatians 5:22–23), and whom you know to be serious students of the Bible.

Consulting the Spiritually Mature

This brings us to another group we may wish to consult: those in our communities of faith who are spiritually mature and devoted to the study of Scripture. We might ask such people how they understand this passage, and how they try to take Jesus' words seriously. Perhaps we are unsure that we can reach a point at which we no longer feel anger toward other people, but we may, with God's help, work through our lives to diminish the feelings of anger, extend understanding to other people, and find a sense of peace. How have these mature Christians in our community managed this? Have they found it difficult? What practices, such as prayer, fasting, or meditation, have they put in place to obey this teaching of Christ? What has worked and what has not? What has been most difficult? Within our churches and networks of Christian friends, there is wisdom to be found, wisdom born out of the lived experience of the Christian life.

While drawing on the resources of our own congregations or denominations is important, it can also be helpful to learn from people who practice the Christian faith differently than we do. There are spiritually mature people who practice Christianity differently than the way it is practiced in your or my local church. One of the great joys of my job is that I have had the privilege of worshipping with Christians of many different stripes in many different parts of the world. Roman Catholic; Orthodox; various types of Pentecostals and charismatics, Baptists, and Methodists; non-denominational Christians; Presbyterians; Anglicans; members of the United Church of Christ; megachurches and small churches; rural and urban churches; in places such as Cuba, Israel, Egypt, and Vietnam—God has allowed me to worship alongside this great diversity of brothers and sisters.

One thing I have learned in this process is that biblical interpretation is often affected by context. Your life circumstances come to bear on the way in which you interpret the Bible. It has been made abundantly clear to me that my own North American, Midwestern, United Methodist context represents a very small slice of the Christian world, and many Christian communities interpret the Bible very differently than the community of my home church. Do I always agree with the other interpretations of the Bible that I hear? Of course not. But they help me to see the God of the Bible from different angles and in a new light. No Christian community has a monopoly on the Bible, and we can all learn from one another. Each one of us can, to some extent, purposefully engage Christians who see things differently than we do. We will thereby enrich our understanding of the Bible and the Christian life.

Consulting Believers Who Have Gone before Us

It can also be helpful to consult not just the present community, but the community of believers who have gone before us in the faith. Of course, this includes the biblical writers themselves, and different parts of the Bible can illuminate one another. Let's return for a moment to the matter of insult raised by Matthew 5:21–22. There are other passages in the Bible that can help us to develop a Christian understanding of the way in which we should speak to and about one another. Consider, for example, Titus 3:2, which instructs us "to slander no one, to be peaceable and considerate, and always to be gentle toward everyone." This is no less of a difficult instruction than Jesus gives us in Matthew. Of course, we can be peaceable and considerate toward some people, even most people, but toward everyone? This is indeed a goal of the Christian life that the Bible sets out for us, but we know that we may not always live up to this ideal. As James teaches us, "We all stumble in many ways" (3:2). Nevertheless, the consequences of unchecked speech are significant. James teaches us in the same passage that "the tongue is a small part of the body, but it makes great boasts. Consider what a great forest is set on fire by a small spark. The tongue also is a fire, a world of evil among the parts of the body. It corrupts the whole body, sets the whole course of one's life on fire, and is itself set on fire by hell" (3:5–6). No wonder both Jesus and Paul are so demanding when it comes to the monitoring of our speech. If we consider the words of James, we know that he is right: with our language, we can do considerable damage if we are not careful.

Apart from the biblical writers, there are great thinkers in the history of our faith who have reflected on the very same issues we confront today. Some have left extensive bodies of writing that can help us as we think about God and the ways in which we are called to live. For example, Augustine wrote,

> Thus let us understand, my dearly beloved, that if no human being can tame the tongue, we must take refuge in God, who will tame it. . . . Consider this analogy from the animals we tame. A horse does not tame itself; a camel does not tame itself; an elephant does not tame itself; a snake does not tame itself; a lion does not tame itself. So too a man does not tame himself. In order to tame a horse, an ox, a camel, an elephant, a lion and a snake,

a human being is required. Therefore God should be required in order for a human being to be tamed.[6]

We cannot on our own, said Augustine, hope to control our own speech. We are by nature wilder, more unruly than we think. We will inevitably speak in ways we should not unless God works in our lives to tame our tongues, the way one might tame an animal. If this sounds like a harsh assessment, consider how often we encounter gossip, slander, profanity, and insult—even within the family of faith. We know that we should avoid such speech, but we engage in it nonetheless.

Another of our forebears in the faith who wrote about the potential evils of speech is John Wesley. In 1760, he wrote a sermon called "The Cure of Evil-Speaking." Wesley has great insights on the sin of evil-speaking, by which he means speaking ill of another person when he or she is not present. He noted how common this sin is, and how it is found among all manner of people. Because it is so common, he said, we have lost our sensitivity to it. We may not even notice it when we encounter it. This sin indulges our pride and anger, he noted. We even fool ourselves into believing that we are justified in calling out the sins of others, that we may thus speak out of a sense of righteous indignation.

Wesley then pointed us to another passage in the Bible that provides practical advice on this matter: "If your brother or sister sins, go and point out their fault, just between the two of you" (Matt. 18:15). When you do so, you should not do so pridefully, as if you are better than the other person. You should avoid any hint of hatred or ill will. Rather, your words should be gentle in the hope of winning the other person over. It is possible in certain circumstances to convey your message through another person, if you trust the messenger to keep the matter between the three of you. It is also possible to write to the other person. The preferred way of doing things, though, is to speak with the other person yourself.

What if the other person will not listen? Wesley then urged us on to the next verse in Matthew: "But if they will not listen, take one or two others along" (18:16). These should be people who love both God and neighbor. They should be gentle and patient, and not the kind of people who are quick to retaliate.

Only after the first two steps should we make this matter public to other members of the church. "If they still refuse to listen, tell it to the church" (Matt. 18:17). Wesley wrote that the best way to do this is to consult the elders of the church, and to do it in the presence of the person concerned. Again, this should be done in a spirit of love.

If and only if this third step fails to bring about repentance in the person who has offended, we should then "treat them as you would a pagan or a tax collector" (Matt. 18:17). What does this mean? According to Wesley, it means, "You are under no obligation to think of him any more—only when you commend him to God in prayer. You need not speak of him any more, but leave him to his own Master." Nevertheless, our Christian obligations do not end at this point. "Indeed you still owe to him . . . earnest, tender goodwill. You owe him courtesy, as an occasion offers all the offices of humanity. But have no friendship, no familiarity with him."[7]

Wesley's sermon represents the reflection of a Christian person who spent his life immersed in prayer and Scripture. He was deeply devoted to living a life of holiness and spent considerable time reading the works of other Christians. He wanted to develop sound, biblical advice for the people called Methodists on how they should live in the way that was most pleasing to God. His advice is not perfect, but like so many other Christian thinkers through the centuries, we can learn a great deal from his insights.

We started this section by looking at Matthew 5:21–22, which raises the matters of anger and insult. We looked briefly at what the scholarly community might think about certain aspects of this passage. We examined the importance of consulting our present community, as well as Christians from different communities. Then we looked at what a few other passages in the Bible might say about these topics. Finally, we consulted a couple of Christians from the past whose wisdom has long been respected among other believers. All of this is part of the process of interpreting the Bible for the life of faith. If we don't wish to interpret for the life of faith, but for some other reason, we could probably stop after we have consulted the scholarly community. But if we want to read the Bible in ways that build up our faith, we need the wisdom of the saints, both past and present. This is not something we do in an afternoon. It is part of a practice, a habit of walking with God using Scripture as our guide.

The Bible and the Creeds

At times in the past, Christians have developed short statements of faith to guide believers in their understanding and proclamation of the good news of Jesus Christ. Some churches, such as the Roman Catholic Church, the Orthodox Church, the Anglican Church, and some Methodists and Presbyterians are explicit in their use of the historic creeds. The most commonly used are the Nicene Creed and the Apostles' Creed. Some Protestant churches, especially those that practice more informal or contemporary forms of worship, have what might be called an "implicit creed." For example, in these churches, you would likely learn that God is the Holy Trinity, and that Christ was fully God and fully human. These beliefs, summarized for the church in historic creeds, have made their way into the theology of these Christian traditions, even though the creeds themselves have not. Rather than preserving these beliefs in the form of a creed, these communities pass them down through preaching, music, and teaching.

Occasionally I have heard people claim that their church or denomination is non-creedal. I don't believe that there is any such thing as a non-creedal church. There are churches with implicit creeds and churches with explicit creeds. Every Christian tradition, however, is organized around some set of beliefs that set it apart from other traditions, and the adherents of those traditions generally know what those beliefs are. These beliefs help to shape the ways in which the community of faith understands and applies Scripture.

Why are the creeds important? They are important because they summarize for us the story of God's saving work on our behalf. This story tells us what God has done in the past, including the creation of the universe, the coming of God's Son to save us from sin, and his crucifixion and resurrection. It also tells us of what God is doing in the present as the Holy Spirit abides among the community of the church. Finally, it tells us what God is going to do in the future by raising the dead, judging all people, and receiving the faithful into eternal life.

This is the story of our salvation, which has a beginning, middle, and an end. In various forms, it has been preserved to teach Christians about the nature of God and what God has done for us. As Christopher Bryan wrote, "Insofar as our biblical canon as a whole has a 'matter,' this creedal story, this Rule of Faith, is it."[8] In other words, the Bible tells us a story that is summarized in our historic creeds. Insofar as we understand this story, we grasp the central ideas about God's creating and saving work on our behalf. It is easy to misinterpret Scripture, even if we have the best of intentions, and the creeds help to make good theological sense of what we read in the Bible.[9]

The second-century Christian bishop Irenaeus wrote a work called *Against Heresies*. He was dealing with forms of early Christianity that he felt did not sufficiently express the basic content of the gospel. Those people with whom Irenaeus took issue, however, were most often using exactly the same sacred texts as he was. The problem was not that they were using the wrong texts, but the way in which they interpreted them. Irenaeus said that the Bible is like a mosaic that depicts a king. Some people, however, come along and rearrange the pieces of the mosaic so that, rather than a king, it depicts a fox. In other words, they cause the writings of Scripture to testify to something other than that which God has done for our salvation.[10]

Reading through parts of the Bible, for example, like the Gospel of John, we might begin to wonder about Jesus' full humanity. Yes, John's Jesus is certainly divine. We learn this in some of the first verses of the Gospel: "In the beginning was the Word, and the Word was with God, and the Word was God. . . . The Word became flesh and made his dwelling among us" (John 1:1, 14). This Word, who was God, became flesh . . . but what does this mean? Christians in the past have wrestled with this very issue. And almost all churches of both the East and the West have assented to the statements of the Nicene Creed on this issue:

> For us and for our salvation
> He came down from heaven,
> was incarnate of the Holy Spirit and the Virgin Mary
> and became truly human.
> For our sake He was crucified under Pontius Pilate;
> He suffered death and was buried.
> On the third day He rose again
> in accordance with the scriptures;
> He ascended into heaven
> and is seated at the right hand of the Father.

Jesus was incarnate. He was made human. He also suffered and died. He was not an angel or simply a spirit, but a person. Even after the Nicene Creed was finalized, however, Christians continued to struggle with the difficult issue of the relationship between Jesus' divinity and humanity. To address ongoing questions and disputes, theologians developed the Definition of Chalcedon (which is basically another creed), and like the Nicene Creed it was adopted broadly throughout the church. The Definition specifies that Jesus was "perfect in Godhead and also perfect in manhood; truly God and truly man," and that he was "in all things like unto us, without sin." Jesus, then, was entirely divine, and he was also entirely human. He was no less of one than the other. Without the guidance of the church, we might miss this point. If we don't have in hand some of these basic concepts about who Jesus was and what God did through him, we are bound to misunderstand many other aspects of our faith.

These creedal teachings of the church provide some helpful parameters for our interpretation of Scripture. The Bible is really too large, and its subject matter too vast, for any one of us to interpret on our own. Therefore, we read with the communion of saints, both past and present. The church's creedal tradition provides helpful and concise material born out of the struggles between earnest Christians attempting to understand the nature of our God and our salvation through Jesus Christ. As we walk the pathway into the life of God, the saints who have gone before us have left markers along the way.

Conclusion

Reading the Bible isn't like reading a newspaper or website from which we simply derive information and opinions. Reading the Bible is a spiritual practice that draws us more deeply into the life of

God. In life, we are often enriched by hearing and thinking through the ideas of other people, no matter what the subject matter. Yet it is particularly important that we do so with the Bible because its subject matter—the saving work of God among men and women— is too deep, too rich and vast for any one of us. In fact, it is too great for all of us together to understand. Nevertheless, we will go much more deeply into the life and mysteries of God if we seek the wisdom of other people, particularly others who are walking with us along the path of faith.

Reading the Bible in community can be a lot of work. It involves time and effort, including reading the works of people who have invested themselves in biblical scholarship. It requires patience, humility, and an openness to the insights of other people. We must be humble enough to listen—really listen—to those among our community of faith who are fellow pilgrims walking alongside us on this journey toward God. And it is crucial to bear in mind that our family of faith consists not only of those people who sit beside us in church, but the communion of saints who have gone before us, faithful women and men who have given their lives to God. In the long history of the church, there is immeasurable accumulated wisdom. To avail ourselves of this wisdom may at times be labor intensive, but consider the reward: to know and love God more fully, and to understand God's great love for us.

CHAPTER 3 STUDY QUESTIONS

1. Who in the community of faith do you turn to for wisdom and guidance?
2. Who or what do you consult for understanding in biblical interpretation?
3. How might learning from those who practice Christian faith differently than you benefit your interpretation of Scripture?
4. In this chapter, we discussed that a unique interpretation is usually incorrect. Why is it important to compare your beliefs to the commonly accepted beliefs held by the Christian community at large today and in the past?
5. Read through the Nicene or Apostles' Creed. What are the fundamental teachings of Christianity in these creeds? How do these core teachings instruct how you read Scripture?

CHAPTER 4

EXPECTATION AND THE LIFE OF GOD

My friend and colleague Kent Millard once told me about a very powerful experience of healing he witnessed. When he described his view of miracles up to that point in life he said, "I think I was exceedingly rational, and thought that things spoken of in the Bible probably had another explanation rather than the miraculous. There was some rational explanation for everything. Jesus walking on water—it *looked like* he was walking on water. The feeding with fives loaves and two fish means that everyone brought a lunch and shared with everyone else." He would look for "any way to explain away the miraculous." He continued, "With regard to healing, I think I remember a professor once saying that when someone prayed and someone thought they were healed it was just psychological manipulation. That is, they thought they were healed because they were so positive, or believed that they felt better, but they weren't really healed."

Later in his life, he met an Australian pastor named Rev. John Blacker. The two were working together on a common project and, as Kent wrote in his book, *The Gratitude Path*, "Rev. Blacker believed strongly in the power of God to heal through prayer and took seriously Christ's command to 'heal the sick.'"[1] While Blacker was in town, a woman in Kent's congregation called the church. She wanted to know if he would come to her house and pray over her husband, who suffered from terrible back pain. He had seen many different doctors, but nothing seemed to help. She was a believer, but her husband, she explained, was not.

The two men went to the house together and found the man sitting in a recliner. He was clearly in pain. When Kent introduced them and said that they were there to pray for his healing, the man responded, "I'd do anything to get some relief from this pain."[2] Kent explained what happened next,

> Rev. Blacker went around behind him, laid his hands on his shoulders, and simply prayed, "God, thank you for this healing." Then he stood there with his hands on the man's shoulders praying silently for about ten minutes.
>
> I saw tears running down the man's cheeks. After a while Rev. Blacker prayed again, "God, thank you for this healing."
>
> We sat in silence for a few moments and then the man opened his eyes, got up out of his chair, walked around the room, and simply said, "It's gone. The pain is gone." We joined hands together and offered a prayer of thanksgiving to God.

Now Kent had a problem. His experience didn't match his theology. He had one of two choices. He could reject what he saw or change his theology. He chose the latter. "This experience had a profound effect on me and my ministry," he wrote.

> After this experience, whenever someone asked me to pray for them or for someone they loved, I would stop whatever I was doing, take their hand in mine, and offer a brief prayer requesting God's healing for them or their loved one. . . . I want to be available to request God's healing power any time or any place prayer is requested.[3]

Over his forty-seven-year career in pastoral ministry, Kent has had many opportunities to pray with people, and he has seen the power of God at work many more times. He told me,

> Those kinds of experiences just made me realize that if that kind of miracle could happen through our prayers, then every miracle in the Bible could have happened. Why would I say, 'This miracle happened,' but Jesus couldn't have walked on water? Or Jesus couldn't have been born of a virgin? Or Jesus couldn't have been resurrected, or couldn't have raised the dead? It's like, the experience here [in his own life] confirmed the miracles there [in the Bible].

Kent's experiences taught him to believe in the ways that God is described as acting in Scripture, and the Scripture continued to teach him about the kinds of works that God can and will do in the world today. He came to know God in a new way, a more personal way. After that, he expected more when he prayed. He listened more closely for God's voice. God took on a new reality for him, and he was drawn more closely into the divine life.

Scripture expands our vision outside of the world that we can see and touch. It teaches us about the intersections between the world of spirit—God's world, a world of angels, demons, and eternity—and our own existence as flesh-and-blood beings in this material world. The Bible teaches us to expect more of God than we normally do. It leads us to think about God as someone who acts directly within history. Not everyone will receive the Bible in this way, though. There are certain habits of thinking, particularly in Western culture, that prevent our belief in the active presence of God in this world. In this chapter, we will look at the ways in which our beliefs about the Bible affect our beliefs about God's work in the world today, and vice versa. We will also look at the works of

God, both in Scripture and today, as means of God's self-revelation to build up the church. By receiving God's gifts, we can be drawn more deeply into the divine life. Finally, we will look at miracles in relationship to human suffering.

Active and Passive Disbelief

From the eighteenth century onward, belief in the biblical God—a God who acts directly within history—has fallen on hard times. The stories in the Bible that recount events such as Elijah's raising of a boy from the dead, Peter's healing of a man unable to walk, and even Jesus' resurrection were understood as the product of an ancient worldview, and not something that modern people could believe in. This ancient worldview also included belief in angels, demons, and the afterlife. The great biblical scholar Rudolf Bultmann once said, "We cannot use electric lights and radios and, in the event of illness, avail ourselves of modern medical and clinical means and at the same time believe in the spirit and wonder world of the New Testament."[4] Bultmann believed that the worldview of the New Testament, one in which people were miraculously healed, angels and demons existed, and people got up from the dead, was simply unbelievable. He called this a "mythical" worldview, and argued, "it is impossible to repristinate a past world picture by sheer resolve, especially a *mythical* world picture, now that all of our thinking is irrevocably formed by science."[5]

Bultmann, of course, was not alone in this perspective. He represented a much wider school of thought, which was extremely influential among many theologians, pastors, and laypeople. Yes, they would say, we do believe in God, and we believe that Jesus has something very important to say in our lives. The stories in the Bible, though, about healings, angels, demons, Jesus' virginal conception, and his resurrection from the dead are simply unbelievable to us today. They are ancient myths from which we can learn, but not historical accounts of actual events. This *active disbelief* in the supernatural involves a clear commitment to a worldview that excludes direct acts of God and the existence of a wider spiritual world. C. S. Lewis once wrote that he was suspected of being a fundamentalist because "I never regard any narrative as unhistorical simply on the ground that it includes the miraculous."[6] While not a professional theologian, however, Lewis was not afraid to swim against the scholarly current. "The real reason why I can accept as historical a story in which a miracle occurs is that I have never found any philosophical grounds for the universal negative proposition that miracles do not happen."[7] This is one of the many ways in which Lewis stands out as a Christian intellectual in his day.

I was once sitting in on a course for people new to our church taught by an old, much-beloved pastor in a congregation I was serving. One of the people in the course asked if United Methodists believe in an afterlife. I suppose this person could have been asking about "going to heaven" after we die, or perhaps about the Christian claim that God will raise us from the dead on the last day. Regardless, this pastor thought for a moment and said, "Well, I don't." I almost fell out of my chair. Here was a United Methodist minister, charged with teaching people about the core content of our faith, and yet denying our eternal life with God. He had modernized Christian teaching so entirely that he had given up on the notion that there is more to our lives than this short sojourn on earth.

I worked alongside this man. He was truly kind, and people loved him for it. He would visit the sick. He would give to the poor and serve those in need. He was a fine orator and his sermons evoked a compassionate spirit in other people. He certainly understood that the Christian life is one of self-giving and service. But he had been so formed by the skeptical theological traditions of his day that he did not have the intellectual space to believe in a God who could or would raise the dead into eternal life. He actively disbelieved this faith claim. His position wasn't just "wait and see," or, "I believe in something, but I don't know what." It was, "No, there is no life after this one." His understanding of the Christian faith came from an era in which extreme skepticism had permeated the religious academy and much of the mainline church. Sadly, both the church and his theological education had failed him.

There is yet another kind of disbelief, which I would call *passive disbelief.* That is to say, while being open to the possibility of accounts of miraculous healing, angels, and the resurrection from the dead, many people keep a kind of cool distance from these beliefs. Their attitude is, "Sure . . . why not?" Yet the idea that God might show up in their lives in powerful, redeeming ways does no heavy lifting in their everyday expectations of God, their prayer lives, or the way they might talk about God to other people. They may not want to seem weird or fanatical, or perhaps they simply don't have time in their lives to think deeply about what kinds of things God might really want to do for them and those they love. Their faith lives may revolve around taking their kids to church and religious holidays like Christmas and Easter, but they do not anticipate anything truly life-changing to come out of their religious observances. They might pray before meals or before going to bed, but they don't pray for things that could only be explained by the powerful presence and work of the Holy Spirit. While different than those deeply formed by skepticism, they nevertheless keep at arm's length the picture of God revealed to us in Scripture.

I believe that both active and passive disbelief are problems in the church today. I'm not suggesting we should be utterly uncritical in our beliefs or that we should accept every claim about a miracle or divine encounter that comes down the pike. Rather, my point is that we should not only be open to the kinds of acts that God performs in the Bible, but actively seek them.

The Gifts of the Spirit

Several years ago I had the privilege of meeting Randy Clark. Randy was the principal preacher during the Toronto Blessing, a massive revival that began in 1994 and launched him into international prominence. He now leads a powerful Christian renewal movement called Global Awakening. I have seen incredible things happen through Randy's ministry. One of the key points that he usually makes when he speaks about God's work in the world is that we should expect more of God than we do. We should have, he said, a *culture of expectation* in our churches. We should *expect* God to be generous with the gifts of the Spirit. What are these gifts? Paul talked about them in 1 Corinthians 12:7–11:

> Now to each one the manifestation of the Spirit is given for the common good. To one there is given through the Spirit a message of wisdom, to another a message of knowledge by means of the same Spirit, to another faith by the same Spirit, to another gifts of healing by that one Spirit, to another miraculous powers, to another prophecy, to another distinguishing between spirits, to another speaking in different kinds of tongues, and to still another the interpretation of tongues. All these are the work of one and the same Spirit, and he distributes them to each one, just as he determines.

Most Christians are entirely comfortable talking about gifts of wisdom and faith. But healing? Miraculous powers? Prophecy? These may be harder to believe—but why? Simply put, the less a particular gift seems to require of God, the easier it is for us to believe. We have been taught not to expect very much of God, and our prayers match those expectations. We may or may not actively disbelieve in these gifts, but passive disbelief in them is quite common.

Let's take an example out of the history of the Methodist movement. Virtually everyone who has belonged to some Methodist or Wesleyan body for any period of time has heard about John Wesley's Aldersgate experience. In his journal entry dated May 24, 1738, Wesley wrote:

> In the evening I went very unwillingly to a society in Aldersgate Street, where one was reading Luther's Preface to the Epistle to the Romans. About a quarter before nine, while he was describing the change which God works in the heart through faith in Christ, I felt my heart strangely warmed. I felt I did trust in Christ, Christ alone for salvation, and an assurance was given me that He had taken away *my* sins, even *mine*, and saved *me* from the law of sin and death.[8]

Here we might say Wesley received the gift of faith. He would call it "assurance," but that is simply another word for faith in Christ for the redemption of his sins.

Now let's look at a lesser-known story in which Wesley mentioned a Mr. Meyrick who came down sick at the same time as Wesley. While Wesley recovered, Mr. Meyrick did not. His health continued to decline, and eventually he died. The story, however, does not end there. Wesley wrote:

> When I came home they told me the physician said he did not expect Mr. Meyrick would live till the morning. I went to him, but his pulse was gone. He had been speechless and senseless for some time. A few of us immediately joined in prayer. (I relate the naked fact.) Before we had done his sense and his speech

returned. Now he that will account for this by *natural causes* has my free leave. But I choose to say, This is the power of God.[9]

When I first came across this passage, I was astounded. Here is a claim by John Wesley that he and other people prayed for a man who was dead, and the man was thereby restored to life! In fact, there are many other supernatural events that Wesley recounted throughout his ministry that we rarely hear about.[10] Why is it that we celebrate Wesley's Aldersgate experience so widely, but these other events in Wesley's life rarely see the light of day? Perhaps it is because the story in which Wesley felt his heart "strangely warmed" is simply more believable to us than the claim that a dead man was restored to life through prayer. To put it a bit differently, the gift of faith is more palatable to our modern sensibilities than the working of miracles.

There are precedents in Scripture for Wesley's prayer over the deceased Mr. Meyrick. Through prayer, Elijah raises the son of the widow at Zarephath (1 Kings 17:17–24). Jesus raises the daughter of a ruler (Matthew 9:18–19, 23–26). When Eutychus falls out of a window to his death during a long-winded sermon by Paul, the apostle embraces him and pronounces that there is life in him, and Eutychus is restored to life (Acts 20:7–12). If we allow Scripture to shape our understanding of the world, we will be more likely to see truth in Wesley's story than to dismiss it out of hand. Wesley certainly had his moments of doubt, but he also lived in expectation of what God was going to do. His image of God as one who acts powerfully in the everyday lives of men and women was formed by the Bible. He believed that God would change the hearts of people who did not have faith. He believed God would enliven the faith of those who lived in doubt. He believed that God could and did heal the sick, and even raise the dead. Wesley expected God to show up because that is how God is described in the Bible.

What if, rather than assenting to the pessimism that so character-izes secular culture, we allowed the Bible to shape our expectations? Scripture teaches us that God *wants* to give us the gifts of the Spirit because these gifts serve the *common good*. In other words, God wants to build up the church and therefore offers us these powerful gifts of the Spirit. The journey into the life of God is not primarily an indi-vidual undertaking. It is something that we do as members of Christ's body in communion with other believers. These gifts are given for our common good, so that, as a community of Christians, we can grow in the faith, know God more fully, and love God and other people more completely. The gifts of the Spirit described in Scripture draw us as the people of God into the life of God. If we are not open to them—or to the idea that God is willing and able to provide them—we impoverish ourselves spiritually. We deprive ourselves of important resources for knowing God and entering into the divine life.

The Works of God as Revelation

Scripture teaches us about the ways in which God has worked in ages past. Scripture also teaches us about the ways in which God wishes to work in our lives today. By learning about God's work through Israel, Jesus Christ, and the early church, we also learn about the character of the God we serve. The works of God are a form of divine revelation, and the most significant of the works of God are related in the Bible. In fact, what Christians and Jews call the "history of salvation" involves example after example of divine action. Think of the exodus from Egypt, the giving of the Jewish law, the inspiration of the prophets, the incarnation of God in Jesus Christ, his virginal conception, and his resurrection from the dead. The biblical God is a powerful, intentional agent, and the works of God teach us about the divine nature and character.

The Bible is full of stories of the mighty acts of God, and these mighty acts are of many different kinds and for many different purposes. Again and again, Scripture tells us of a God who enters into the messy details of human life. Think of the stories of Moses, Jacob, and Mary. Think of times when Jesus heals the sick and casts out demons, as do his followers after him in the Acts of the Apostles. Paul recounted an appearance of Christ to him. John of Patmos saw visions of heaven, angels, martyrs, a dragon and beasts, and a new heaven and earth. There is nothing distant about the God of the Bible. This God is intimately involved in human affairs. Jesus tells us that God knows the number of hairs on our heads (Luke 12:7). The biblical God is at times a creator, a warrior, a rescuer, an inspirer of prophets, a healer, and a redeemer. The biblical God is an actor, an agent, a do-er, one who shows up within everyday life, within the cause-and-effect nexus of history. To reject the notion of God as one who acts in this world is to give up the history of salvation of which we read in the Bible.

Let's look at a specific biblical example of the way in which Christ's powerful divine action reveals a deeper truth about his identity and mission. Mark 2:1–12 tells a story in which people bring Jesus a paralyzed man for healing. Rather than healing the man immediately, Jesus said to him, "Son, your sins are forgiven" (2:5). Some of the scribes who were there grumbled within their hearts and inwardly accused Jesus of blasphemy. He perceived their thoughts, however, and said to them, "Why are you thinking these things? Which is easier: to say to this paralyzed man, 'Your sins are forgiven,' or to say, 'Get up, take your mat and walk'? But I want you to know that the Son of Man has authority on earth to forgive sins" (2:8–10). Therefore, he said to the paralyzed man, "I tell you, get up, take your mat and go home" (2:11). The man immediately got up and left, and everyone was amazed. The point of this story is not that Jesus healed the man's disability by forgiving his sin. We are not intended to believe that the sin was causing the paralysis. Rather, the point is that Jesus does have divine authority, both to forgive sins and heal the sick. The authority for each of these actions is the same, and it comes from the same source. One is visible and one is not. The visible action of healing demonstrates that Jesus has the divine authority he claimed when he pronounced forgiveness of the paralyzed man's sins. Christ used this healing to reveal deeper truths about himself. There are likewise many places in the Bible that teach us about God's authority, power, and love, if only we will take seriously the images of God given to us in our Scriptures.

Learning from the Global Church

Once I was talking with a good friend about the idea of miracles. My friend at the time was an agnostic. When I told him that I believed in miracles such as Jesus' healing of a leper and his bodily resurrection, my friend responded, "I believe in a world governed by the laws of nature." *Well*, I thought, *so do I*. If I drop a stone out of a window, the stone will fall to the ground because of the law of gravity. We would both agree on this. The real question was not whether we believed in the laws of nature, but whether we believed in a God who would work through or circumvent those laws. To be clear, my friend wasn't denying outright the existence of God, but rather questioning the reality of a God who acts in this world in observable, even dramatic ways.

Many of us in the West regard the universe as a closed system. If God exists, God does not interfere within this closed system. The world operates according to particular laws of nature, quite apart from any divine action. We need to understand, however, that we represent a minority report. All throughout history, human beings have engaged with what Philip Jenkins called an "unseen world."[11] If we look at forms of Christianity today in places like China, Latin America, and Africa, we will often witness Christian expression that models its expectations on the biblical stories of God's mighty works, and which is not encumbered by the skepticism one so often finds in Western Christianity.

I once had a conversation with a Filipino Christian who told me how strange it was that so many North American Christians were uncomfortable with phenomena like exorcism and miracles. Where he came from, he said, these things happened quite commonly and were generally accepted as valid. In places where Christianity is thriving throughout the world, places like Africa, Asia, and Latin America, there is a deep and abiding belief in the supernatural. Indeed, for many Christians outside of the United States and Western Europe, biblical miracles provide a template for their expectations of God today. Much like the people of whom we read in the Bible, these Christians believe in the presence and action of God and of angelic and demonic beings. As Jenkins wrote, "If there is a single key area of faith and practice that divides Northern and Southern Christians, it is this matter of spiritual forces and their effects on the everyday human world."[12] Beliefs and practices of exorcism, spiritual warfare, prophecy, and particularly healing are part and parcel of Christianity throughout the two-thirds world. Jenkins continued, "In this thought-world, prophecy is an everyday reality, while faith-healing, exorcism, and dream-visions are all fundamental parts of religious sensibility."[13]

The first time I took a group of students to Cuba, our first worship experiences with the Methodists there were a bit of a shock. It was simply expected that we, as a group consisting of seminary teachers, pastors, and future pastors would lay hands on the sick and pray for their healing. I had some experience with this. Most of my students had none. We were simply called up, however, to lead prayers for healing and the impartation of gifts. We all got some serious on-the-job training. What likely surprised many people in my group was that we did, in fact, see miracles take place. The expectations of the congregations were shaped by their reading of Scripture, and people came forward with the full expectation of experiencing the Holy Spirit. We might have had only the faith of a mustard seed in what we were doing, but the people for whom we prayed were full to the brim with faith in the power of God. They knew the stories of the Bible, and they knew what God can do.

We in the West might be tempted to ascribe such belief to a lack of education or intellectual sophistication throughout the developing world. This would be a mistake. As I have interacted with churches in places like Vietnam and Cuba, I have noticed how well-educated many of these pastors are. Some are doctors, engineers, or teachers. This could be said of many people in the congregations as well. No, not all are so highly educated, but neither are all pastors and parishioners in the United States. Simply to ascribe belief in the supernatural to a lack of intellectual sophistication is really a manifestation of the arrogance of the modern Western world. The reason for more common belief in direct divine action among people in the developing world than in the West is likely that people in the developing world are more acutely aware of their need for God. Comfortable, self-satisfied people are generally content to give up on the idea of a God of power. Those who live from day to day, who must rely on the goodness and power of God, are not. Indeed, Jesus tells us that it is easier for a camel to go through the eye of a needle than for a rich man to enter the kingdom of heaven (Matthew 19:24). Perhaps this is because the rich are so often kept from acknowledging their utter dependence upon God, their human frailty, their sinfulness, and the ephemeral nature of their lives. (It is worth noting here that we who live in the United States are often among the richest people in the world. We do not always think of ourselves in this way, but the mere availability of food, electricity, and clean water places us in an economic station above most people around the globe.) In places where God is wanted and needed, God shows up. God shows up in miracles of healing, prophecy, words of knowledge, and wisdom. These things happened in the Bible, and they are happening today all around the world. I have seen them myself.

Miracles and the Problem of Suffering

I am in no way suggesting in this chapter that God will, in this life, solve our every problem. Nor am I suggesting that, if we only have enough faith, God will grant our every wish. One very common and powerful objection against belief in divine action is that there is so much suffering in the world.[14] If miracles take place, they do not take place all of the time. Is God simply capricious? Why does God act in one case and not in another? As Craig Keener wrote in his book *Miracles: The Credibility of the New Testament Accounts*, "My personal questions today are not whether God heals people, sometimes in demonstrable ways. My struggles now are for the vast numbers of people in the world—probably the majority—who need healing in some sort or another and do not have it, most of whom have little access to medical help."[15]

My guess is that you have prayed fervently at times, and things still did not work out how you would have wanted. That is certainly the case for me. To be very honest, I don't understand God. I don't comprehend God's ways. I have been confused by God, and even angry at what seemed to be divine absence. At other times, however, I have been astounded at what God has done. I've seen God create possibilities where there were none. I've seen God heal the sick. I've seen God change hearts that I never thought would change. Perhaps you've seen God at work in your life as well. If we're going to give so much weight to the times when God does not answer our prayers in the way we would like, we also have to take into account the times when God does show up in powerful, delightful, even life-changing ways. Keener continued his account of his own wrestling with the questions of miracles and human suffering. Because of the profundity of his insights on this matter, I will quote him at length:

> The universality of human mortality demonstrates that even the most optimistic construal of miracles will not eradicate human suffering; miracles do not always occur. The physical benefits that they confer when they do occur are necessarily temporary, but in the context of the Gospels' theology, they are also signs of a better, eschatological kingdom for all who hope in Jesus. In the full context of Jesus' ministry, such signs reveal a kingdom that also involves suffering and is currently overshadowed by the cross, the necessary gateway to the resurrection. They function as promises of a better future, of ideal wholeness, because they reveal the God of the cross, who understands and embraces suffering and can be trusted to be found even there. As signs of kingdom power, however, the miracles foreshadow the hope that lies beyond the cross. While Jesus' unjust execution unveils the world's injustice, his ministry to the broken summons his followers to address the same concerns on which Jesus acted.[16]

The world that we live in is broken, and while we should expect the blessings of God, we should also expect the brokenness of the world to come to bear on our lives. Advances in medicine and technology, the fact that people in the modern West live longer than ever, decreases in infant mortality rates, and other such positive developments can give us a false sense of security in this broken and sinful world in which we live.[17] In wealthier nations, many of us have the capacity to shield ourselves from life's harshest realities much of the time. We rarely see death up close. Our babies are born in hospitals and our children are immunized. The stores in which we shop always have food. But then, inevitably, we are brought back to reality. We receive a bad diagnosis. A man with a gun starts shooting in a church. A tornado touches down and destroys a community. Life is, as Frances Young put it, both "brokenness and blessing."[18]

It is worth noting that, while testifying again and again to the works of God in this world, the Bible also takes notice of times when God seems absent, unfair, or mysterious. We might ask, like the psalmist, "Why, LORD, do you stand far off? Why do you hide yourself in times of trouble?" (Ps. 10:1). Consider also the first two verses of Psalm 13:

> How long, LORD? Will you forget me forever?
> > How long will you hide your face from me?
> How long must I wrestle with my thoughts
> > and day after day have sorrow in my heart?
> How long will my enemy triumph over me?

Job, in his distress, lamented and wished for days when it seemed God was with him:

> How I long for the months gone by,
> > for the days when God watched over me,
> when his lamp shone on my head
> > and by his light I walked through darkness!
> Oh, for the days when I was in my prime,
> > when God's intimate friendship blessed my house,
> when the Almighty was still with me
> > and my children were around me,

> when my path was drenched with cream
>> and the rock poured out for me streams of olive oil.
> (Job 29:2–6)

Belief in divine action does not mean that we put on rose-colored glasses and expect that the kingdom of God will now arrive in its fullness. No, we live in the in-between time. We live in the time after Christ, but before the uniting of heaven and earth. We live in a time of both good and evil, joy and pain. That is the nature of our lives. That is the biblical witness: that we see now through a glass darkly (1 Corinthians 13:12), and God's ways remain in so many ways mysterious to us. We will suffer disappointment again and again if we expect that, in this life, God will solve every problem and right every wrong. Yet we will miss many blessings of God if we simply say that, because of hurt, suffering, and problems, divine action must be a myth. We live in the tension between the hardship of life and the blessings of God. This tension is evident again and again in the pages of the Bible. There is crucifixion, but there is also resurrection. There is persecution, but there is also the spread of the gospel. In Christ, God entered into the suffering of human life, and in the Holy Spirit, God still abides with us today. Hurt, blessings, sorrow, and joy: that is the life described time and again in the Bible, and it is the reality of the world in which we live.

Conclusion

One of the most commonplace teachings of the Bible is that God enters into human affairs, takes a personal interest in us, and acts in ways that surprise, challenge, and delight us. Relegating these to the category of myth is to do a tremendous disservice to ourselves and other Christians, and it is to misrepresent the character of God. The biblical God is one who acts. If we do not receive this God in our reading of the Bible, then we worship a god of our own invention, one who can never truly surprise or delight us, who is confined simply to the limits of our own imagination. That is not the God of the Bible.[19]

Rather than a culture of skepticism, we should try to create a culture of expectation in our churches. We should wait *expectantly* for God to work in our midst. This does not mean that God will solve every problem or heal every illness, but rather that God *will* in fact work in remarkable, sometimes dramatic ways, in the very day-to-day fabric of our lives. We should *wait* in expectation. We should *pray* in expectation. And we should *read* in expectation. When we read about God's works among the people of Israel, Jesus, and his first followers, this can help us to understand who God is and how God works. In many churches, creating a culture of expectation will require changing the atmosphere quite dramatically. Then again, God can do that too.

CHAPTER 4 STUDY QUESTIONS

1. What does Scripture tell us about the miraculous?
2. Why do you think the miraculous is common in other parts of the world, but considered strange in the West today?
3. Do you believe God is still presently active in this world, acting powerfully in the lives of men and women? How has God acted in your life?
4. Would you say that you have an active or passive disbelief in the supernatural, or do you believe in the supernatural?
5. Are you open to the idea that God is willing and able to provide gifts of the Spirit? If not, what or where is the source of resistance? If you are, how can you continue to cultivate openness to God's provision of gifts of the Spirit?

CHAPTER 5

ONE BOOK FOR THE LIFE OF GOD

When I was a teenager, a friend of mine and I decided to go to the movies together. I checked the time the movie started and picked him up, but I was running a little late. The movie had already started by the time we go there. We sat down and tried to catch the drift of what was happening, but the longer we sat, the less the movie made sense. We looked at one another quizzically, wondering how we'd missed so much in the brief time since the movie started.

About ten minutes later, the movie ended and the credits began to roll. We weren't just a few minutes late. We were about an hour-and-a-half late. I'd gotten the time wrong.

So after I'd received considerable ridicule from my friend in the best tradition of teenage boys, we waited for the movie to start over and watched it from beginning to end. This time the last ten minutes made a lot more sense. We had the whole story.

Reading the Bible is much the same. The Bible tells us a story. It begins with creation, and it ends with new creation. In the middle it tells of humankind's rebellion against God, the birth of a chosen people, the back-and-forth of human faithfulness and faithlessness, and the call of the prophets. It culminates in the life, death, and resurrection of Jesus, and it reflects on life after Jesus ascended into heaven. The more we know of this story, the more we can comprehend its meaning. If we only attend to certain parts of the story, we will miss the fullness of its meaning for our lives, our churches, and ultimately all of creation.

John Wesley called himself "a man of one book."[1] This one book was, of course, the Bible. Wesley was clear that the Old and New Testaments are not two books, but one. Neither do the sixty-six books contained within our Bible stand alone.[2] They are not to be read in isolation from one another, but in light of one another. Yes, each individual book of the Bible has a particular witness, but that particular witness is part of a greater whole, a larger story. Wesley understood the importance of reading the whole Bible, and he instructed his preachers to do so. We would do well to follow his lead.

Another way of saying that the Bible is one book is to say that the Old and New Testaments together form a canon of Scripture. In this chapter we are going to look at what it means to think of the Bible as canon. The Greek word *kanōn* means "rule" or "measuring rod." These books together represent the set of writings that the church has historically authorized to teach the faith to the people of God.[3] The two Testaments of the canon help to interpret one another, and one is incomplete without the other. If we have only the Old Testament or only the New Testament, we miss out on the fullness of God's story.

Two Testaments, One Bible

Have you ever heard someone say, "I don't like the God of the Old Testament," or, "I'm a New Testament person, not an Old Testament person"? Christians have made this remark from very early on in the history of our faith. In the second century, a Christian leader named

Marcion decided that the God described in the Old Testament was simply irreconcilable with what followers of Jesus should believe about God. The God of the Old Testament, he claimed, was inferior to the Christian God revealed in Jesus. Even many Christian writings, such as the Gospel of Matthew, were simply too "Jewish" for him. Therefore, Marcion developed what we call the "Marcionite Canon," which consisted of edited versions of the Gospel of Luke and some of Paul's letters. It contained no Old Testament; aspects of the selected New Testament writings that seemed too Jewish to him were edited out.

Thankfully, most of our forebears in the faith understood that Marcion's canon represented a huge theological mistake. The God of the Old Testament is also the God of the New Testament. The God who came to us in Jesus is the same God who led Israel out of Egypt and gave her the law, raised up and brought down kings, and spoke to and through the Old Testament prophets. This is the God about whom Jesus taught and to whom Jesus prayed. The basic set of writings that we call the Old Testament was for Jesus and the writers of the New Testament, the Scripture.

Reading through the Bible, moreover, one can see that the God of the Old Testament is not without compassion, and the God of the New Testament is not without wrath. Consider the words of Psalm 103:8–13 in the Old Testament:

> The LORD is compassionate and gracious,
> > slow to anger, abounding in love.
> He will not always accuse,
> > nor will he harbor his anger forever;
> he does not treat us as our sins deserve
> > or repay us according to our iniquities.
> For as high as the heavens are above the earth,

so great is his love for those who fear him;
as far as the east is from the west,
    so far has he removed our transgressions from us.
As a father has compassion on his children,
    so the LORD has compassion on those who fear him.

Consider also these words of Jesus from the Gospel of Matthew 7:21–23:

> Not everyone who says to me, "Lord, Lord," will enter the kingdom of heaven, but only the one who does the will of my Father who is in heaven. Many will say to me on that day, "Lord, Lord, did we not prophesy in your name and in your name drive out demons and in your name perform many miracles?" Then I will tell them plainly, "I never knew you. Away from me, you evildoers!"

This is not gentle Jesus, meek and mild. This is a Jesus who rejects those who refuse to do the will of God, who sends them away into punishment. If this sounds a lot like the actions of the Old Testament God, that's because the God who came to us in Jesus, and about whom Jesus taught, is the God of the Old Testament. There is one God, revealed to us throughout the entirety of the story of our salvation.

God and the Unity of Scripture

Much of the Bible is made up of smaller stories. Think of Genesis, Exodus, and Ruth. Think of the four Gospels and the Acts of the Apostles. These are stories or collections of stories. Together, they form part of the larger story of salvation. There are, of course, parts of the Bible that are not written as stories, such as Psalms, Proverbs, Ecclesiastes, Romans, and Hebrews. These books help us to interpret the story of salvation by reflecting on the character of God, God's saving work in history, and the human condition. By reading the story given to us in Scripture, we learn about the God who saves. We encounter a God we do not understand. We confront the good and bad aspects of our own lives, and we learn more about the people around us. Consequently, we draw closer to God, entering more fully into the divine life, and God in turn shapes us into more Christlike people.

The unity between the two Testaments and among the many books of the Bible is not simply the result of the work of people who selected the right books and excluded the wrong ones. The unity of the Bible is first and foremost the result of the power and work of the Holy Spirit.[4] The Bible came to us *through* people, but it came to us *from* God. As the theologian Kevin Vanhoozer wrote, to think about the canon of Scripture as a unified work is to suggest a divine intention behind its unity. We will miss the completeness of the Bible unless we understand that its completeness is the result of the work of God.[5] In other words, the reason we read the different parts of the Bible in light of one another is that God intends for us to do so. It is not simply the church that has given us the Bible; it is God. The Bible, then, is not just a collection of *works*; it is a *work*.[6] The writings of the Bible function collectively to teach us about the faith and lead us into the life of God.

The Diversity of Scripture

Have you ever closed your eyes, opened your Bible, and put your finger down on a random passage, just to see what you would end up with? You could land on a passage like . . .

> Judges 3:21–22: "Ehud reached with his left hand, drew the sword from his right thigh and plunged it into the king's

belly. Even the handle sank in after the blade, and his bowels discharged. Ehud did not pull the sword out, and the fat closed in over it."

Or . . .

Song of Solomon 4:2: "Your teeth are like a flock of sheep just shorn, coming up from the washing. Each has its twin; not one of them is alone."

Or, maybe . . .

Mark 14:51–52: "A young man, wearing nothing but a linen garment, was following Jesus. When they seized him, he fled naked, leaving his garment behind."

If you give this experiment a try a few times, the wide and varied nature of the biblical writings will no doubt become apparent in short order. The people who wrote, edited, and compiled the Bible lived in different parts of the world, spoke different languages, and lived in different historical eras. They had different experiences and thought about the world in different ways. Therefore, it is to be expected that within the Bible we will encounter a variety of perspectives on the nature of God, the work of God in the world, and the ways in which human beings should respond to God. As Beth Felker Jones put it: "When we read the [Bible], we see that the Spirit, in inspiring the Scriptures, did not erase or smooth over these differences between the human authors of the texts."[7]

For example, the Bible contains different viewpoints on the relationship between righteousness and prosperity on the one hand, and sin and ruin on the other. Sometimes the Bible teaches that a life lived righteously before God will be a happy and prosperous life, and that a life of sin will lead to all kinds of calamity. At other times, biblical writers seem less sure of this connection.

They observe that sometimes righteous people suffer, and sometimes sinful people prosper.

A few examples will illustrate the differences. In Deuteronomy 7:12–16, God told the people of Israel that if the people of Israel would obey God and keep his covenant, he would bless them. "He will bless the fruit of your womb, the crops of your land—your grain, new wine and olive oil—the calves of your herds and the lambs of your flocks in the land he swore to your ancestors to give you" (7:13). Just as obedience will produce fruitfulness, however, disobedience will invite God's wrath: "If you ever forget the LORD your God and follow other gods and worship and bow down to them, I testify against you today that you will surely be destroyed. Like the nations the LORD destroyed before you, so you will be destroyed for not obeying the LORD your God" (Deut. 8:19–20).

We find a similar idea, though in more general terms, in Proverbs 3:33–35:

> The LORD's curse is on the house of the wicked,
>   but he blesses the home of the righteous.
> He mocks proud mockers
>   but shows favor to the humble and oppressed.
> The wise inherit honor,
>   but fools get only shame.

This is a great idea, but it simply isn't true all the time. Sometimes bad things happen to good people, and good things happen to bad people. My father-in-law, whom I never met, was by all accounts a devout Christian. He was very active in his church. He was a devoted family man and worked as an accountant for the Church Pastoral Aid Society. He died at the age of forty-seven from kidney failure caused by a congenital condition. Before his death he had been ill for several years and required regular dialysis. He left behind a family with four children, the youngest of whom is now my wife. She was nine years old when he died. His story doesn't fit the righteousness-equals-prosperity perspective we see in Deuteronomy, Proverbs, and other parts of the Bible.

Within the Bible itself, though, there are writings that push back against the direct link between righteousness and reward, sinfulness and ruin. The entire book of Job is a reflection on the question, Why do righteous people sometimes suffer? Job, after all, is said to have been "blameless and upright; he feared God and shunned evil" (1:1). Yet this blameless and upright man lost his property and children, his health, and the respect of his wife and friends. In one of his speeches, Job asked a question that directly confronts the perspective we have seen in Deuteronomy and Proverbs: "Why do the wicked live on, growing old and increasing in power?" (21:7). Why, he wants to know, do they get to spend time with their children, when he does not? Why are their houses safe? Why do they get to enjoy happiness?

Job, who had lived righteously, wanted to make his case before God. He wanted to ask what he did wrong:

> Even today my complaint is bitter; his hand is heavy in spite of my groaning. If only I knew where to find him; if only I could go to his dwelling! I would state my case before him and fill my mouth with arguments. I would find out what he would answer me, and consider what he would say to me. (23:2–5)

God did, in fact, respond to Job's complaint, though not as Job would have liked. The response was, in a nutshell, "You have no idea what you're talking about." Were you there, God asked, when I created the earth? Have you ever been in the depths of the sea or seen the gates of death? Do you understand the secrets of the natural world? If not, how can you possibly expect to find fault with the almighty God? Job responded simply by admitting that he was wrong: "Surely I spoke of things I did not understand, things too wonderful for me to know" (42:3).

At the end of the story, Job's fortunes are restored twofold, but the question of the suffering of the righteous stands wide and gaping. The book of Job never answers the question of why the righteous suffer or the wicked prosper. It simply asserts that they do, and in the process dismantles simplistic connections between righteousness and prosperity, sinfulness and suffering. It seems that the book of Job is, in fact, wrestling with other parts of the Bible, even arguing with them.

The book of Ecclesiastes also observes that things sometimes go badly for the righteous and well for the wicked. "In this meaning-less life of mine I have seen both of these: the righteous perishing in their righteousness, and the wicked living long in their wicked-ness" (7:15). The same idea again occurs shortly thereafter: "There is something else meaningless that occurs on earth: the righteous who get what the wicked deserve, and the wicked who get what the righteous deserve. This too, I say, is meaningless" (8:14).

To take simply one of these perspectives, that righteous-ness leads to prosperity, or that suffering is basically random, inexplicable, and meaningless, leads us to an overly simplistic understanding of the relationship between righteousness and blessings, sin and suffering. On the one hand, we can end up affirming a prosperity gospel in which God's blessing of health and wealth awaits the righteous. The problem here is just what Job and Ecclesiastes have pointed out: experience shows that the direct correlation between righteousness and prosperity does not always hold, and this kind of belief can lead to bad financial deci-sions, false expectations, and a loss of faith. On the other hand, liberal Protestant traditions tend to focus on the suffering in this world to the point that the concept of blessing, and particularly material blessing, is no longer meaningful for them. The problem of suffering leads them to a theology in which blessing does no heavy lifting. They resonate with Job's complaint, perhaps not on their own behalf, but on behalf of the many who suffer throughout the world today. They get the perspective of Ecclesiastes and empathize with the perplexity it expresses. But a God who does not bless, who does not enter into the everyday lives of men and women in powerful ways, is not the biblical God. The Bible offers us varied perspectives on the topics of righteousness, sin, blessing, and suffering—perspectives that are consistent with the variety of human experiences of God.

To recognize the diversity of perspectives in Scripture in no way undermines the authority of the Bible or the truthfulness of the Christian witness. In fact, it enriches it. If God had wanted us to have a book with no internal tensions and disagreements, in which one part always agreed with another part, that is the book we would have. But that is not the book we have. In fact, the book we have serves us much better than one in which everything fits together like pieces of a jigsaw puzzle. The eternal God, who created all things, who has no beginning and no end, who transcends both time and space, is not a God who can be neatly packaged. The eternal God is ultimately beyond our ability to comprehend. A god who is ultimately comprehensible is not the Christian God. Such a god would be too small, too weak, and too simple to be the God revealed in Scripture.

The Bible and Scripture: Two Different Things?

Apart from the fact that the Bible does not always agree with itself, however, there is another complicating factor. The Bible some-times represents perspectives that seem incomprehensible to us as Christians. This can create internal conflict and confusion for us—what might be called a bad case of ethical heartburn. We are committed to the reading of the Bible, but we are also committed to a certain moral life not always represented in the Bible. Take, for example, the last two verses of Psalm 137:

> Daughter Babylon, doomed to destruction,
>> happy is the one who repays you
>> according to what you have done to us.
> Happy is the one who seizes your infants
>> and dashes them against the rocks.

If we are sometimes shocked when we come across a passage like this one in the Bible, it may well be *because* we have been properly formed as Christians. Part of being a Christian involves understanding that, in the universe God created, there is right and there is wrong, and if the church has done its job, we will usually know it when we see it. Our faith teaches us that revenge is wrong. It most certainly teaches that such brutality to infants is wrong. Any properly formed Christian will believe these things. So when confronted with a text like this, we might well exclaim, *"That's in the Bible?!?"*

The Jefferson Method

In my experience, the way that most Christians deal with these kinds of passages is by ignoring them. This is what might be called the "Jefferson method." Thomas Jefferson produced his own rendition of Jesus' teachings by cutting out (literally) the parts of the New Testament he believed were inconsistent with reason, much of which had to do with the New Testament miracles. He then pasted together (literally) his own rendition of Jesus' teachings that expressed what he considered to be a reasonable moral philosophy. Christians today do this as well, though we normally do not use a knife, paper, and paste. We tend to say something like, "Well, that passage was fine for folks in those days, but today we know better," or, "That passage simply reflects an ancient worldview with ancient morals, and we need not pay any attention to it today." Surely, we think to ourselves, the parts of the Bible dealing with love, kindness, and eternal life are inspired, but these other parts simply can't be. Therefore, while the Bible we read still contains the same number of books, chapters, and verses it always has, *functionally* we have abbreviated the Bible and relegated large sections of it to a pile of "uninspired" passages. We don't need them because, well, we know better now.

What I am calling the "Jefferson method" is quite similar to the position advocated by Adam Hamilton in *Making Sense of the Bible*. Hamilton argued that we may divide Scripture into three broad categories (for which he uses the analogy of "buckets"). He wrote that some passages of the Bible *"reflect the timeless will of God for human beings."* Others *"reflect God's will in a particular time but not for all time,"* (for example, much of the ritual law of the Old Testament). Still others *"reflect the culture and historical circumstances in which they were written but never reflected God's timeless will."*[8] In suggesting this approach, Hamilton was attempting to address passages of Scripture that many readers today find difficult, such as those that state that women should be silent, that slaves should obey their masters, or that same-sex intimacy is sinful.

Biblical Rules and the Principles behind Them

I believe that Hamilton has accurately described the way in which many mainline Christians today read the Bible, though they are not usually so explicit about doing so. This approach to the Bible, however, is laden with difficulties. Take, for example, the idea that some passages of

Scripture were important for a particular time and place, but no longer reflect God's will. A good example might be Deuteronomy 22:8: "When you build a new house, make a parapet [wall] around your roof so that you may not bring the guilt of bloodshed on your house if someone falls from the roof." At least in Western culture, most people don't spend much time on the roof. It's not a major concern for us that someone might fall off the roof, as it was in the ancient world when the roof of a house might be used as a place of leisure. So is this passage one that reflected God's will at one time, but does so no longer? We might be tempted to send it to the second bucket.

Gordon Fee and Douglas Stuart, however, described one way in which this passage is still significant for readers today: "If we are not concerned about building parapets around the roof of our houses (Deut. 22:8), we should nonetheless delight in a God who cared that houseguests not fall off a (usually flat) roof with which they were unfamiliar; and therefore God's people were taught to build their houses with that sort of love for neighbor in mind."[9] While the exact command is not particularly relevant to us today, then, the principle behind it is: we should demonstrate our love for our neighbors by the way in which we live our daily lives. Were we to identify this passage as one that reflected God's will for a particular time but does so no longer, we would miss what it can teach us about God's will for our lives today. There are undoubtedly many other passages of Scripture similar to this one, as culturally specific expressions of broader principles related to God's will for our lives.

Did God Inspire Only Part of the Bible?

As for the third bucket, Hamilton argued that some passages of the Bible have never reflected God's timeless will. This is simply another way of saying that parts of the Bible are not inspired. Following this argument to its inevitable conclusion, we will have to affirm that *there are parts of the Bible that should not function as Scripture*. If a biblical text can in no way be said to reflect God's will, then surely God does not want us guided by that text. God would not have given us such a text. It follows that God did not inspire it. Can we reasonably call it Scripture if it does not reflect God's will and is uninspired?

It is helpful here to return to the definition of "Scripture" from Castello and Wall cited in the introduction: "'Scripture' signals a way of thinking theologically about the Bible as God's Word for God's people, one that supplies the theological goods that fund spiritual wisdom and provide moral direction."[10] Applying this definition to Hamilton's method, the "second bucket" passages were at one time God's Word for God's people, but are no longer. Thus while they remain within the covers of the Bible, we can no longer call them Scripture. The "third bucket" passages were *never* God's Word for God's people. If they never reflected God's will, they do not provide useful or truthful theological goods. They do not fund spiritual wisdom or provide moral direction. In essence, they never have been Scripture. By this account, the Bible and Scripture are two different things.

Another concern I have with this method is that, if we divide Scripture into these three categories, our perspectives become the measuring rod or rule by which Scripture is judged, and not the other way around. We have thus lost the sense of Scripture as canon. If you and I are to judge which passages of the Bible reflect the will of God and which do not, we will eventually end up with an abbreviated Bible that is no more than a reflection of the comfortable theological, philosophical, and moral positions of a particular time and place. Scripture will no longer be able to challenge our assumptions about God, humankind, and the relationship between the two. We have taken away from the Bible the authority to challenge the theological and moral assumptions we bring to our reading. We have taken from it the capacity to lead us to repentance.

Learning to Learn from Scripture's Hard Passages

To be clear, I am *not* arguing that we should ignore the real moral problems that come up as we read through the Bible. There are a few things to consider here. First, not every passage in the Bible is *prescriptive*. Some are simply *descriptive*. As my pastor once said in a sermon, the Bible does not *sup*port everything it *re*ports. When the biblical writers describe human behavior, they don't flinch. They don't shy away from the depth of human sin or the brutality with which people sometimes treat one another.

Second Samuel 11 tells a story in which King David slept with Bathsheba, the wife of one of his soldiers, Uriah. When he learned that Bathsheba was pregnant, David tried to get Uriah to sleep with her so that he would think that he (Uriah) had fathered the child. Uriah would not do so, even though he was a Hittite, because the Israelite rules of war forbade it. Further, it would have dishonored his fellow soldiers. Eventually, David had Uriah killed. The story is laden with serious ethical problems. Even though David was one of the great heroes of the Bible, here we encounter him as a deceitful and treacherous ruler who would murder a loyal soldier for his own gain. This story underscores one of the most common themes of the Bible: the human rebellion against God, and the terrible consequences of this rebellion. People sin, and the biblical writers describe this sin very well. By engaging passages that depict the tendency to sin, we can learn important truths about the nature of human life.

Thus some passages describe human sin, but also condemn it. Yet what about passages of the Bible that condone moral perspectives that we see as inconsistent with the Christian life? Let's return to the example of the last two verses of Psalm 137:

> Daughter Babylon, doomed to destruction,
>> happy is the one who repays you
>> according to what you have done to us.
> Happy is the one who seizes your infants
>> and dashes them against the rocks.

This psalm describes the feelings of Judean people taken into captivity in Babylon. They were angry. They missed their homeland. The land God promised to their ancestors had been taken from them. The last two verses are particularly brutal. They show us the desire for revenge. The invaders who showed no mercy deserved no mercy themselves, a principle that extended even to the infants among them.

As noted above, this perspective is inconsistent with our faith. Jesus taught us to forego revenge, to love our enemies and pray for those who persecute us. Yet even though we do not support the moral perspective of the text, there is, in fact, a great deal we can learn from it. While it is not God's will that we take violent revenge against our enemies, it is God's will that we recognize our own tendencies toward wrath, the seeds of vindictiveness that lie within us, and the commonplace human desire to get even with those who have hurt us. It is also God's will that, having identified and named these tendencies and desires, we engage the wider canon of Scripture for the well-being of our own souls and the formation of our character as Christians. There are many parts of Scripture, both in the Old Testament and the New Testament, that present perspectives on revenge that are quite different than the one we find in this psalm.

We need to pay attention to these as well. No passage of Scripture stands on its own. All of it stands within the broader canon.[11]

Another issue made clearer by engagement with the breadth of the biblical witness is the leadership of women in the life of the church. I was once teaching a group of students in my seminary's doctor of ministry program. These students represented several different Christian traditions, including United Methodists, Pentecostals, Episcopalians, and non-denominational Christians. The topic of women in ministry came up, and I stated my belief that God does call women into ministry, just as God calls men into ministry. An extremely bright and talented woman in the class raised her hand and asked about the very pointed instruction regarding women in the church in 1 Timothy 2:11–15:

> A woman should learn in quietness and full submission. I do not permit a woman to teach or to assume authority over a man; she must be quiet. For Adam was formed first, then Eve. And Adam was not the one deceived; it was the woman who was deceived and became a sinner. But women will be saved through childbearing— if they continue in faith, love and holiness with propriety.

She was distressed because, like me, she held a high view of Scripture, and I think she was concerned that this passage called into question her own work of ministry.

Many Protestant Christians, including many evangelicals and Charismatics, have affirmed women in ordained ministry for quite some time. In light of passages like 1 Timothy 2:11–15 (and others such as 1 Corinthians 14:34–35), the question arises as to whether or not such groups are defying Scripture in their practices. How can these Christians who hold Scripture in such high regard affirm the leadership, ministry, and ordination of women? Wouldn't this passage simply preclude leadership and teaching by women?

It will not do simply to say that passages like this one represent an ancient worldview, that we know better now because we have progressed in our moral understanding beyond the perspectives of the biblical writers. God worked through ancient people to give us the Bible. The entire Bible thus reflects the perspectives of ancient people. If we are going to dismiss passages that reflect such perspectives, we will lose our entire canon of Scripture. Many scriptural concepts such as love, honor, grace, and holiness had specific meanings for ancient Mediterranean people that never even occur to modern Westerners. Nevertheless, Christians persist in using these concepts quite freely today, often in very different ways than the writers of our Bible would have envisioned. Understanding the historical and cultural contexts of passages of Scripture can help us to avoid distorting the meaning of a text. It can help us to develop faithful interpretations that we can apply to our lives today. In and of itself, however, the historical distance between the cultures of the Bible and our cultures today does not determine the function of a passage of Scripture for present-day communities of faith.

A more helpful approach to this passage and others like it is to read it within the context of the broader canon of Scripture. Our Bible does not offer us one clear perspective on the leadership of women. Rather, it offers a variety of perspectives, in part by depicting women as leaders in different roles in different contexts.[12]

Let's look at two different examples from the Old Testament. Deborah is said to have been both a prophet and a judge—a leader of the people of Israel before the establishment of the monarchy (see Judges 4:4). Under her leadership, Israel secures a great victory over the forces of Sisera. The Song of Deborah celebrates, "Villagers in Israel would not fight; they held back until I, Deborah, arose, until I arose, a mother in Israel" (Judg. 5:7). The female prophet Huldah, likewise, must have occupied a place of high importance among the

Israelites. When Josiah read the newly discovered book of the law, he instructed members of his court to "Go and inquire of the LORD for me and for the people and for all Judah about what is written in this book that has been found" (2 Kings 22:13). Though there were other prophets in Israel at the time, they chose to go to Huldah, a woman, for this important task.

There are also New Testament examples of women providing important leadership. It is no small thing that the first people to go and tell of the resurrection were women. Although women were not considered reliable witnesses in the Greco-Roman world, Matthew testified that an angel instructed the women to go and tell that Jesus had risen (Matthew 28:7), and that Jesus himself gave the same instruction (see Matthew 28:10). In the Gospel of John, it is Mary Magdalene who told the disciples of the empty tomb. She was also the first person to whom Jesus appeared after his resurrection, and the first person who told the disciples that Jesus was alive. Prisca (Priscilla) is said to be one of the people who instructed Apollos about the way of the Lord, and particularly about baptism. This must have been rather advanced instruction since Apollos had already received instruction elsewhere and was said to have been knowledgeable about Scripture (see Acts 18:24–28). Phoebe is said to be a "deacon of the church" (Rom. 16:1) and even 1 Timothy, with its harsh instructions about the necessary silence of women, seems to make provisions for women to serve as deacons (see 3:11–13).[13] The exact function of a deacon in the early church is unclear, though the mention of deacons alongside bishops in Philippians 1:1 indicates that this was a position of some importance. Junia, mentioned in Romans 16:7, appeared to have been an apostle, and Paul wrote that, along with Andronicus, they were imprisoned together. First Corinthians 11:6 references the public prayers and prophecies of women among the community of faith.

The cultures in which the Old and New Testaments came into being were without question patriarchal in comparison to our own. In spite of this, we see in the Bible a number of instances of women occupying crucial leadership roles both in Israel and in the early church. These exceptions to the general rules of ancient patriarchal societies show us that God empowers women for all kinds of ministry through the gifts of the Spirit. The complexity of the scriptural witness means that we cannot simply point to a single passage as normative for the way in which we understand gender roles in the church.

What, then, of the passages that do appear to limit the roles of women in the church? What should we do with 1 Timothy 2:11–15? The early church, like the church today, struggled with many different challenges. One was the ordering of the life of the church. Another was the necessity of getting by in the Greco-Roman world. It seems that this passage from 1 Timothy, along with other passages such as 1 Corinthians 14:34–35, are attempts to maintain order in the life of the church and a peaceable relationship with non-Christian neighbors. Paul would not forbid women to speak in church if they were not already doing so. It may be that the utterances of some women in the Spirit were interrupting the community's worship. It may also be that the unconventional behavior of Christian women was beginning to raise suspicion of Christians among their non-Christian neighbors. In the Greco-Roman world, women were often prohibited from speaking in public.[14] Where they were allowed to speak in public, many people still disapproved of their doing so.[15] Their public speech in Christian contexts may have caused difficulties with non-Christian neighbors, who would have seen them as upsetting the established social order. Paul, then, may be giving situation-specific instructions in both of these passages. The wider canon of

Scripture, however, does not support making these instructions into universal rules.

The whole Bible is inspired, but this does not mean, however, that every passage of Scripture is equally important, or that every passage of Scripture tells us directly how we should live. We come to understand the significance of various parts of Scripture by their relationship to the Bible's story of salvation. This story teaches that God loves us, that God wants us to live righteously, that we sin against God, and that God has sent Jesus in the ultimate act of salvation. Rather than asking which passages of Scripture we may rightly ignore, perhaps we should ask how a given passage relates to God's story of salvation. Does it show us how God wants us to live as people saved from sin and death (love your enemies)? Does it show a negative example—how we should *not* live (like the story of David and Bathsheba)? Does it depict the sinful tendencies of humankind or emotional responses that can lead us into sin (like the end of Psalm 137)? Does it teach us about God's great love for us ("For God so loved the world . . ." [John 3:16])? Different parts of the Bible can serve us in different ways. The diversity of Scripture and the inspiration of Scripture fit together hand in glove.

The Divine and the Human in Scripture

In his book, *Reflections on the Psalms*, C. S. Lewis noted how very *human* the writings of Scripture sometimes seem. Take again the example from Psalm 137, or the remark in 2 Peter 2:12 regarding false teachers: "They are like unreasoning animals, creatures of instinct, born only to be caught and destroyed, and like animals they too will perish." Even those Christians who are most committed to the establishment of sound doctrine will wince at a

SCRIPTURE AND THE LIFE OF GOD

statement like this one. Regarding passages of Scripture such as these, Lewis wrote:

> The human qualities of the raw materials show through. Naïvety, error, contradiction, even (as in the cursing Psalms) wickedness are not removed. The total result is not "the Word of God" in the sense that every passage, in itself, gives impeccable science or history. It carries the word of God; and we (under grace, with attention to tradition, and to interpreters wiser than ourselves, and with the use of such intelligence and learning as we may have) receive that word from it not by using it as an encyclopedia or an encyclical but by steeping ourselves in its tone or temper and so learning its overall message.[16]

What is noteworthy here is his insistence on the human element in the writings of Scripture. The works that together make up our Bible are inspired by God, but God gave them to us through human beings. Human beings are not perfect. We are broken by sin, mortal, and limited in our vision. While giving us access to God through divine revelation, then, the works of Scripture necessarily bear the marks of their human authors. Lewis called this "an untidy and leaky vehicle."[17] Nevertheless, this is the vehicle that God has chosen. Even as he wrote of the "naïvety, error, contradiction," and "wickedness" that one encounters in Scripture, Lewis affirmed that Scripture leads us into salvation.

In fact, he said, our wrestling with Scripture, the struggle to work our way beyond the limitations of the human authors and truly encounter God, can lead us to greater heights than if we never had to struggle in this way:

> Certainly it seems to me that from having had to reach what is really the Voice of God in the cursing Psalms through all the horrible distortions of the human medium, I have gained

something I might not have gained from a flawless, ethical exposition. The shadows have indicated (at least to my heart) something more about the light.[18]

Scripture as Self-Correcting

How do we handle, then, the variety of voices in Scripture? How do we make sense of the many different perspectives, the sorrow and elation, the blessing and cursing, law and grace, suffering and blessing? Not to put too fine a point on it, but this is very difficult work. It is the work of a lifetime. We learn from others in our communities of faith. We look to the wisdom of believers past and present. We seek God in prayer. And as we engage the biblical texts time and again, as we hear them read and preached, read them in our devotions, recite them in song, meditate upon them, and internalize them, we will begin to learn the themes of Scripture, to hear one biblical perspective even as we are reading another. We will come to have some limited grasp of the fullness of Scripture, its richness and complexity, even as we become ever more aware of how much more we have to learn.

It is helpful here to turn to the work of James Sanders, who has written with great insight about the different perspectives in Scripture. Different parts of the Bible, he suggested, challenge one another, *and this is a good thing*. Even though they are under divine inspiration, the biblical writers are wrestling with some of the hardest questions that people can ask. When one biblical writer leans too far into one perspective (say, that righteousness will equal prosperity) another will push back and offer a different take on the matter (sometimes the righteous suffer). Sanders called these differences among the biblical texts "redeeming contradictions."[19] One part challenges and illuminates another part. If we think we have God figured out, our certainty will be upended by the variety of voices we encounter in the Bible. Scripture has, then, a "self-correcting" function.[20] In this way, it helps us to engage a wide range of human experiences of God that can speak to the varied experiences we have in our own lives.

We cannot then simply pick passages in the Bible that we should read and those we may ignore. The matter is more complex than this. All of Scripture is of God, and all of Scripture comes to us through human authors, editors, copyists, and translators. While some passages of the Bible are more clearly consistent with what we believe to be the Christian life intended by God than others, it is not our prerogative simply to dispense with the parts of the Bible that are most objectionable to us. We do not claim that every passage of Scripture is equally important, but neither can we call some passages uninspired or suggest that one passage is of God while another passage is simply a human creation. We must use discernment through study, prayer, reflection, and the guidance of the community around us to receive all that we can in our engagement with the whole Bible. John Wesley wrote:

> The Scripture, therefore, of the Old and New Testament is a most solid and precious system of divine truth. Every part thereof is worthy of God; and all together are one entire body, wherein is no defect, no excess. It is the fountain of heavenly wisdom, which they who are able to taste prefer to all writings of men, however wise or learned or holy.[21]

Conclusion

Scripture is not just a collection of writings. It is a single book that is meant to be taken as a whole. It tells us the story of salvation and includes poems, prophecies, collections of wise sayings, and other materials that teach us more about God and his saving work on our behalf. To call the Bible "Scripture" is to affirm that it is inspired— all of it. It is not our prerogative as Christians to decanonize parts of the Bible that we find distasteful or even offensive.

Anyone who has spent very much time in the Bible has come across passages that seem to challenge our vision of the Christian life. There are passages in the Bible that we simply cannot reconcile with what we believe to be Christ's vision for a righteous human life. Nevertheless, even though we are not to understand these passages prescriptively, God can still teach us through them. Perhaps we are to view them as examples of how not to live. Perhaps we can see in them aspects of our own lives, such as anger, jealousy, or greed, that we need to surrender to God in repentance. The Bible expresses a wide range of human experiences, and we can learn from these expressions even while we understand that we should not emulate them all.

While the Bible is inspired by God, it has come to us through human beings. People wrote the stories of the Bible. They wrote the psalms and collected wisdom traditions. They passed down oracles from the prophets and sayings of Jesus. They wrote letters and sermons in the hope of exhorting and admonishing one another. Thus while we receive God's self-revelation in Scripture, we can also perceive at times the marks of human frailty within its pages. There is no point trying to avoid this or being embarrassed by it. This is the way in which God chose to communicate with us for teaching, reproof, correction, and training in righteousness. Our job is not to try to make Scripture into something it is not, but to live faithfully in light of the revelation that God has given us.

There is diversity within the Bible's unity. God is eternal, far beyond our ability to comprehend. There is push and pull within the pages of Scripture. We can learn much from these "redeeming contradictions." As we see the biblical writers engage one another and challenge one another's ideas, so we, too, can engage our own ideas and those of others as we seek to live in righteousness. The diversity within Scripture is not a problem with the Bible, but a gift from God reminding us of the ultimately incomprehensible nature of the divine.

CHAPTER 5 STUDY QUESTIONS

1. Why is it important to know the whole story of the Bible and not just pick one verse?
2. As mentioned in this chapter, some will say, "I don't like the God of the Old Testament," and give preference to the New Testament. How are we able to reconcile the God we see in the Old Testament with the God we see in the New Testament?
3. What are the benefits of the diversity of perspectives in Scripture?
4. How do you handle passages of Scripture that seem shocking, uncomfortable, or difficult?
5. What is the problem with our dividing Scripture into different categories of inspired and uninspired passages?
6. Think of a passage of Scripture you have ignored or find difficult. How does it relate to God's story of salvation? What does it say about God's love or how we should live?

CONCLUSION

We started this book with a story about Augustine, the great theologian of the fourth and fifth centuries whose spiritual autobiography, the *Confessions*, is among the classic works of Christian literature. He would come to be called "Saint Augustine," an iconic figure after whom churches, schools, and cities would be named. Before he was any of these things, though, he was simply a man who came to understand that he needed to know God more deeply than he did. When he heard the voice of a child calling, "Pick up and read," he took it as a sign that God was leading him into the next step of his journey with Christ. He was obedient. He picked up his copy of Paul's letters, he read, and he was transformed. Scripture was the vehicle that God used to lead Augustine across a crucial threshold in his life of faith.

God doesn't reserve these transforming experiences for future bishops and theologians. God wants every single person to receive the life-changing power of the Holy Spirit. God wants each of us to enter into the divine life of the Trinity, to know God and to be known by God. Even for people who have walked in faith for decades, there is still the opportunity to grow in faith, to enter more deeply into the eternal love that exists between the Father, Son, and Holy Spirit. God wants to lift us up out of sin and death, and that is why God has given us Scripture.

Scripture is a pathway into the life of God. People use the Bible for many reasons, but it is meant to lead us into salvation. The

Bible is not properly a weapon of doctrinal disputes. It is not simply an instruction book. It is not "Basic Instructions before Leaving Earth." Our Bible, the Christian Scripture, is first and foremost a way of knowing God. It contains a grand narrative of salvation, though with many twists, turns, and detours along the way. It contains poems and wisdom and prophecies that teach us about this narrative of salvation. As we search the Scriptures prayerfully, as we internalize its words, seeking the guidance of other Christians and the Holy Spirit, we are drawn into God's life. The salvation that is at the center of the biblical witness can be ours as well.

In this book, we have looked at what it means to enter into the life of God through texts that God has inspired and made authoritative for the teaching of the church. We touched on some tricky topics, such as the inspiration and authority of Scripture. If we are to come to know God through Scripture, we should know that Scripture is from God. Because Scripture is from God, we know that it can speak meaningfully into our lives and that we should attend carefully to its teachings. All of Scripture is God-breathed, and it is useful for teaching, reproof, correction, and training in righteousness.

We have looked at ways in which we can avail ourselves most fully of Scripture's treasures. Many of us read the Bible during private devotion time, and this is a very helpful practice, but there are also many other ways to walk down the pathway of Scripture into the divine life. Prayer, meditation, music, corporate worship, and other practices facilitate the work of the Holy Spirit through Scripture in drawing us into the divine life. There is not one right way to engage the Bible. We should use all the means at our disposal to weave the teachings of Scripture into our lives. The church has, through the centuries, passed down to us myriad ways in which we can engage Scripture. By availing ourselves of these practices, we can facilitate the work of the Holy Spirit in our own lives, and enter more fully into the life of God.

Also important is the practice of reading in community. Our faith is not simply an individual faith, but one that we share with believers across the centuries. Other Christians can help us to grow in our understanding of Scripture. They can contribute in important ways to our relationship with God. We should look for people within our communities of faith from whom we can learn, people who clearly know God and are steeped in Scripture. The community of faith, however, consists not only of people living today, but Christians of ages past. They have left us great treasures of Christian wisdom. We tend to view the Bible through the lenses of our own time and place, and Christians from other times and places have blessed us by writing about their own journeys with God through Scripture.

One of the unfortunate tendencies of the nineteenth and twentieth centuries has been the loss of belief in the miraculous, the supernatural. Christian faith stands and falls on the idea that God has acted directly and powerfully in human history, most importantly through the life, death, and resurrection of Jesus Christ. A god who cannot or will not enter directly into the messiness of human affairs is not the God of the Bible. As Christians, we often expect too little of God. It is important, then, to create a culture in which we expect the presence and action of God in our midst.

Finally, we looked at the significance of attending to the *whole* Bible. We cannot simply dispense with the parts of the Bible that we find objectionable. Even though there are parts of the Bible that are not directly prescriptive, we can learn from every part of our sacred, inspired text. Different parts of Scripture function in different ways. All of the Bible is inspired by God, and all of the Bible bears the marks of human authors, editors, and compilers. There are tensions within the Bible—the push and pull of the human endeavor to know and speak about the eternal God. These tensions, the differences in perspective represented in the Bible, are a great help to us. They represent Scripture's self-correcting function.

God is alive. The Christian God is a living God, the essence of whom is love. The Father, Son, and Holy Spirit live forever in an embrace of divine love, and you and I are invited into that embrace. We are invited to receive new life, now and forever. Human beings are broken and sinful, but we don't have to be. God can change us. We can become truly loving people. First John teaches us, "Dear friends, let us love one another, for love comes from God. Everyone who loves has been born of God and knows God" (4:7). When we receive the love of God, we can love other people as we were meant to. We can begin to put away selfishness, conceit, ego, and fear, and live in faith, generosity, and courage. There is nothing more important than knowing God. It is what we are made for. Augustine prayed, "you have made us for yourself, and our heart is restless until it rests in you."[1] How very true that is. Thanks be to God, we have our Scriptures to guide us, to teach us how to find that rest.

NOTES

Introduction

1. Saint Augustine, *Confessions*, trans. Henry Chadwick (New York: Oxford University Press, 1998), 153.

2. John Wesley, "Upon our Lord's Sermon on the Mount: Discourse the First," in *The Sermons of John Wesley: A Collection for the Christian Journey*, eds. Kenneth J. Collins and Jason E. Vickers (Nashville, TN: Abingdon Press, 2013), 1.11.

3. Joel Green addresses a similar issue regarding the relationship between historical study and the church's theological tradition: "Historical study can and should explore the evidence for the Christian claim that Jesus was raised from the dead. But historical study cannot on its own speak to such questions as whether Jesus is God's Son, whether Jesus was the long-awaited Messiah, whether Jesus died for our sins, or whether Jesus' resurrection signaled the restoration of God's people and the ushering in of the new age" (*Seized by Truth: Reading the Bible as Scripture* [Nashville, TN: Abingdon Press, 2007], 167–68).

4. Andrew G. Walker and Robin A. Parry, *Deep Church Rising: The Third Schism and the Recovery of Christian Orthodoxy* (Eugene, OR: Cascade Books, 2014), 42.

5. John Wesley, "The Way to the Kingdom," sermon 6 in *The Sermons of John Wesley: A Collection for the Christian Journey*, eds. Kenneth J. Collins and Jason E. Vickers (Nashville, TN: Abingdon Press, 2013), 1.6.

6. Green, *Seized by Truth*, 150; italics in original.

7. On this topic I highly recommend Joel Green's book *Seized by Truth: Reading the Bible as Scripture* (Nashville, TN: Abingdon Press, 2007).

8. Daniel Castello and Robert W. Wall, "Reading the Bible as Scripture," chapter 1 in *A Compact Guide to the Whole Bible: Learning to Read Scripture's Story*, eds. Robert W. Wall and David R. Nienhuis (Grand Rapids, MI: Baker Academic, 2015), 12.

9. John Wesley, Preface to "Sermons on Several Occasions," in *Sermons I*, ed. Albert Outler, vol. 1 of *The Bicentennial Edition of the Works of John Wesley* (Nashville, TN: Abingdon Press, 1976–), 105–6.

10. See chapter 5, "The Bible as a Book of Meeting," in Christopher Bryan, *And God Spoke: The Authority of the Bible for the Church Today* (Cambridge, MA: Cowley, 2002).

Chapter 1: A Path into the Life of God

1. Kathryn Tanner, *Jesus, Humanity and the Trinity: A Brief Systematic Theology* (Minneapolis, MN: Fortress Press, 2001), 40.

2. Daniel Iverson, "Spirit of the Living God" (No. 393) in *The United Methodist Hymnal* (Nashville, TN: The United Methodist Publishing House, 1989).

3. Athanasius, *On the Incarnation*, 54.

4. Cf. the Roman Catholic statement *Dei Verbum*, which states that Scripture teaches truth that "God wanted to put into the sacred writings for the sake of our salvation" (3:11). See Second Vatican Council, *Dei Verbum* [Dogmatic Constitution on Divine Revelation], Vatican Website, November 18, 1965, ch. 3:11, http://www.vatican.va/archive/hist_councils/ii_vatican_council/documents/vat-ii_const_19651118_dei-verbum_en.html.

5. Richard Dawkins, *The God Delusion* (Boston, MA: Mariner, 2006), 51.

6. Christopher Bryan, *And God Spoke: The Authority of the Bible for the Church Today* (Cambridge, MA: Cowley, 2002), 40.

7. "The [Greek] text is not altogether clear, as the variety of translations shows. There are three major ambiguities: (1) the meaning of *pasa graphē* ('all scripture'), (2) the meaning of

theopneustos ('inspired'), and (3) the grammatical function of *theopneustos*" (Raymond F. Collins, "Inspiration," in *New Jerome Biblical Commentary*, eds. Raymond E. Brown, Joseph A. Fitzmyer, and Roland E. Murphy [New York: Pearson, 1989], 1024). On an alternate translation, which would be rendered something like, "Every inspired Scripture is useful . . ." see Paul J. Achtemeier *The Inspiration of Scripture: Problems and Proposals* (Philadelphia, PA: Westminster, 1980), 106–7.

8. See Collins, "Inspiration," 1025.

9. Cf. Paul J. Achtemeier, *The Inspiration of Scripture*, 107.

10. Achtemeier noted, "Scripture itself apparently thinks it can be inspired as witness to God's saving deeds without having to be regarded as inerrant in matters not central to its witness" (Achtemeier, *The Inspiration of Scripture*, 115).

11. Adam Hamilton, *Making Sense of the Bible: Rediscovering the Power of Scripture Today* (New York: HarperOne, 2014), 294, italics in original. For a critique of this position, see David F. Watson, "Wrestling with Inspiration," review of *Making Sense of the Bible: Rediscovering the Power of Scripture Today*, by Adam Hamilton, *Good News* (July/August 2014): 32–34.

12. When I refer to the biblical writers, I mean to include as well the editors and compilers of materials who gave us the biblical texts in forms more or less like the biblical texts we use today.

13. Achtemeier, *The Inspiration of Scripture*, 116–17.

14. Ibid., 117.

15. I. Howard Marshall, *Biblical Inspiration* (Vancouver: Regent College, 1982), 49.

16. Ibid., 42.

17. Article V of the United Methodist Articles of Religion.

18. Paul J. Achtemeier, *Inspiration and Authority: Nature and Function of Christian Scripture* (Peabody, MA: Hendrickson Publishers, 1999), 146.

19. N. T. Wright, *The Last Word: Beyond the Bible Wars to a New Understanding of the Authority of Scripture* (San Francisco, CA: HarperSanFrancisco, 2005), 114, italics in original.

20. Kenton L. Sparks, *Sacred Word, Broken Word: Biblical Authority & the Dark Side of Scripture* (Grand Rapids, MI: Eerdmans, 2012), 41.

21. John Wesley, "Christian Perfection," sermon 57 in *The Sermons of John Wesley: A Collection for the Christian Journey*, eds. Kenneth J. Collins and Jason E. Vickers (Nashville, TN: Abingdon Press, 2013), 1.9.

Chapter 2: Reading for the Life of God

1. http://www.chrysostompress.org/prayer_before_reading_scripture.html.

2. John Wesley, Preface to *Explanatory Notes upon the Old Testament*, in *Wesley's Notes on the Bible* (Grand Rapids, MI: Francis Asbury Press, 1987), 20.

3. Beth Felker Jones, *God the Spirit: Introducing Pneumatology in Wesleyan and Ecumenical Perspective* (Eugene, OR: Cascade, 2014), 111.

4. Understanding the different functions of inspiration and illumination creates problems for the view of inspiration posited by Adam Hamilton, *Making Sense of the Bible: Rediscovering the Power of Scripture Today* (New York: HarperOne, 2014), 294. They serve different purposes and, therefore, are qualitatively different.

5. See also the description of "illumination" in Craig S. Keener, *Spirit Hermeneutics: Reading Scripture in Light of Pentecost* (Grand Rapids, MI: Eerdmans, 2016), 12–15.

6. Daniel Patte, *Global Bible Commentary* (Nashville, TN: Abingdon Press, 2004), xxii.

7. Richard J. Foster, *Celebration of Discipline: The Path to Spiritual Growth*, 20th Anniversary ed. (San Francisco, CA: HarperSanFrancisco, 1998), 20.

8. Ibid., 29.

9. See Duncan Robertson, *Lectio Divina: The Medieval Experience of Reading* (Trappist, KY: Cistercian Publications, 2011), xiv.

10. Ibid.

11. Justin Martyr, *First Apology*, 67, in *Saint Justin Martyr*, trans. Thomas B. Falls (New York: Christian Heritage, 1948), 106.

12. Reginald Heber, "Holy, Holy, Holy! Lord God Almighty!" *United Methodist Hymnal* (Nashville, TN: United Methodist Publishing House, 1989), #64.
13. Les Garrett, "This Is the Day," © 1967, 1980 Scripture in Song.
14. Brenton Brown and Ken Riley, "Everlasting God," © 2005 Thankyou Music.
15. Episcopal Church, *The Book of Common Prayer and Administration of the Sacraments and Other Rites and Ceremonies of the Church: Together with the Psalter or Psalms of David* (New York: Oxford University Press, 1990), 368.
16. Ibid.
17. Kenneth M. Loyer, *Holy Communion: Celebrating God with Us* (Nashville, TN: Abingdon Press, 2014), 31.

Chapter 3: Guides into the Life of God

1. World Council of Churches, *The Nature and Mission of the Church: A Stage on the Way to a Common Statement* (Geneva: World Council of Churches Publications, 2005), 15, italics mine.
2. "If it is true . . . that the church, by its production of Scripture, created materials which stood over it in judgment and admonition, it is also true that Scripture would not have existed save for the community and its faith out of which Scripture grew" (Paul J. Achtemeier, *The Inspiration of Scripture: Problems and Proposals* [Philadelphia, PA: Westminster, 1980], 116).
3. "Unique interpretations are usually wrong" (Gordon D. Fee and Douglas Stuart, *How to Read the Bible for All Its Worth*, 4th ed. [Grand Rapids, MI: Zondervan, 2014], 22).
4. James A. Sanders, *Canon and Community: A Guide to Canonical Criticism* (Philadelphia, PA: Augsburg Fortress Publishers, 1984), xvii.
5. David Noel Freedman, Allen C. Myers, and Astrid B. Beck, *Eerdmans Dictionary of the Bible* (Grand Rapids, MI: Eerdmans, 2000), 1106.
6. Augustine, Sermon 55.2, in *Ancient Christian Commentary on Scripture: Matthew 1–13*, ed. Manlio Simonetti (Downers Grove, IL: InterVarsity Press, 2001), 102.

7. John Wesley, "The Cure of Evil-Speaking," in *The Sermons of John Wesley: A Collection for the Christian Journey*, eds. Kenneth J. Collins and Jason E Vickers (Nashville, TN: Abingdon Press, 2013), 3.3.

8. Christopher Bryan, *Listening to the Bible: The Art of Faithful Biblical Interpretation* (New York: Oxford University Press, 2014), 68.

9. See the discussion of the role of tradition in shaping biblical interpretation in Joel Green, *Seized by Truth: Reading the Bible as Scripture* (Nashville, TN: Abingdon Press, 2007), 80–88.

10. Irenaeus, Haer. 1.8.1.

Chapter 4: Expectation and the Life of God

1. Kent Millard, *The Gratitude Path: Leading Your Church to Generosity* (Nashville, TN: Abingdon Press, 2015), 51.

2. Ibid., 52.

3. Ibid.

4. Rudolf Bultmann, "New Testament and Mythology" (1941), in *New Testament Mythology and Other Basic Writings*, ed. and trans. Schubert M. Ogden (Philadelphia, PA: Fortress Press, 1984), 4.

5. Ibid., 3, italics in original.

6. C. S. Lewis, *Reflections on the Psalms: The Celebrated Musings on One of the Most Intriguing Books of the Bible* (San Diego, CA: Harvest, 1958), 109.

7. Ibid., 109–10.

8. John Wesley, May 24, 1738, *Journals and Diaries I (1735–1738)*, eds. W. Reginald Ward and Richard P. Heitzenrater, vol. 18 of *The Bicentennial Edition of the Works of John Wesley* (Nashville, TN: Abingdon Press, 1976–), 249–50, italics in original.

9. Wesley, December 20, 1742, *Journal and Diaries II (1738–1743)*, in *Works*, 19:306.

10. See Frank H. Billman's book, *The Supernatural Thread in Methodism: Signs and Wonders Among Methodists Then and Now* (Lake Mary, FL: Creation House Press, 2013).

11. Philip Jenkins, *The Next Christendom: The Coming of Global Christianity*, 3rd ed. (New York: Oxford University Press, 2011), 152.

12. Ibid.
13. Ibid., 10.
14. An excellent study of the Bible as it relates to the problem of suffering is J. Christiaan Beker, *Suffering and Hope: The Biblical Vision and the Human Predicament* (Grand Rapids, MI: Eerdmans, 1994).
15. Craig S. Keener, *Miracles: The Credibility of the New Testament Accounts*, vol. 2 (Grand Rapids, MI: Baker Academic, 2011), 767.
16. Ibid.
17. On this issue, see N. T. Wright, *Evil and the Justice of God* (Downers Grove IL: InterVarsity Press, 2006), 22.
18. See Frances M. Young, *Brokenness and Blessing: Towards a Biblical Spirituality* (Grand Rapids, MI: Baker, 2007).
19. If you have an interest in miracles, and particularly healing, I suggest reading Randy Clark's *Power to Heal: Keys to Activating God's Healing Power in Your Life* (Shippensburg, PA: Destiny Image, 2015).

Chapter 5: One Book for the Life of God

1. John Wesley, Preface to "Sermons on Several Occasions," in *Sermons I*, ed. Albert Outler, vol. 1 of *The Bicentennial Edition of the Works of John Wesley* (Nashville, TN: Abingdon Press, 1976–), 105–6.
2. Seventy-three books for Roman Catholics.
3. On this topic, see David F. Watson, "Scripture as Canon," in *Wesley, Wesleyans, and Reading Bible as Scripture* (Waco, TX: Baylor, 2012), 161–76.
4. Cf. the Roman Catholic statement *Dei Verbum*, which states that Scripture teaches truth that "God wanted to put into the sacred writings for the sake of our salvation" (3:11). See Second Vatican Council, *Dei Verbum* [Dogmatic Constitution on Divine Revelation], Vatican Website, November 18, 1965, ch. 3:11, http://www.vatican.va/archive/hist_councils/ii_vatican_council/documents/vat-ii_const_19651118_dei-verbum_en.html.
5. See Kevin J. Vanhoozer, "Imprisoned or Free? Text, Status, and Theological Interpretation in the Master/Slave Discourse of Philemon," in A. K. M. Adam, Stephen E. Fowl, Kevin J.

Vanhoozer, and Francis Watson, *Reading Scripture with the Church: Toward a Hermeneutic for Theological Interpretation* (Grand Rapids, MI: Baker, 2006), 68–69.

6. See Nicholas Wolterstorff, "The Unity Behind the Canon," in *One Scripture or Many? Canon from Biblical, Theological, and Philosophical Perspectives*, eds. Christine Helmer and Christof Landmesser (New York: Oxford University Press, 2004), 217–32.

7. Beth Felker Jones, *God the Spirit: Introducing Pneumatology in Wesleyan and Ecumenical Perspective* (Eugene, OR: Cascade, 2014), 112.

8. See Adam Hamilton, *Making Sense of the Bible: Rediscovering the Power of Scripture Today* (New York: HarperOne, 2014), 273–74, italics in original.

9. Gordon D. Fee and Douglas Stuart, *How to Read the Bible for All Its Worth*, 4th ed. (Grand Rapids, MI: Zondervan, 2014), 174.

10. Daniel Castello and Robert W. Wall, "Reading the Bible as Scripture," chapter 1 in *A Compact Guide to the Whole Bible: Learning to Read Scripture's Story*, eds. Robert W. Wall and David R. Nienhuis (Grand Rapids, MI: Baker Academic, 2015), 12.

11. For those who want to seriously engage these passages in the Bible that Christians find morally objectionable, I recommend Kenton Sparks, *Sacred Word, Broken Word: Biblical Authority and the Dark Side of Scripture* (Grand Rapids, MI: Eerdmans, 2012), 9.

12. For a helpful overview of Scripture's varied witness on women as leaders, see Valerie Griffiths, "Women as Leaders," in *The IVP Women's Bible Commentary*, eds. Catherine Clark Kroeger and Mary J. Evans (Downer's Grove, IL: IVP Academic, 2002), 642–43.

13. Some interpreters see 1 Timothy 3:11–13 as referring to the wives of deacons. There is no possessive pronoun in this passage, however, to indicate that Paul is referring to the wives of deacons, and the use of "in the same way" (Gk: *ōsautōs*) in verse 11, just as it is used in verse 8, "suggests that a distinct but parallel group of people is being discussed" (Jouette M. Bassler, *1 Timothy, 2 Timothy, Titus* [Nashville, TN: Abingdon Press, 1996], 70).

14. See Korinna Zamfir, "Women Teaching—Spiritually Washing the Feet of the Saints? The Early Christian Reception of 1 Timothy 2:11–12," in *Annali di storia dell'esegesi*, 32, no. 2 (2015): 356.

15. See Craig S. Keener, *1 and 2 Corinthians* (New York: Cambridge University Press, 2005), 118.

16. C. S. Lewis, *Reflections on the Psalms: The Celebrated Musings on One of the Most Intriguing Books of the Bible* (San Diego, CA: Harvest, 1958), 111–12.

17. Ibid., 112. Sparks made a similar, though more detailed, argument in *Sacred Word, Broken Word*.

18. Lewis, *Reflections on the Psalms*, 114.

19. James A. Sanders, *Canon and Community: A Guide to Canonical Criticism* (Philadelphia, PA: Fortress, 1984), 37.

20. Ibid., 46.

21. John Wesley, Preface to *Explanatory Notes Upon the New Testament* (London: Epworth Press, 1976), 9.

Conclusion

1. Augustine, *Confessions*, trans. Henry Chadwick (New York: Oxford University Press, 1991), 1.1.1.

CPSIA information can be obtained
at www.ICGtesting.com
Printed in the USA
LVHW08s1918260718

R13739100002B/R137391PG584157LVX2B/9/P

781628 244724